The Jury Team

During the last eight centuries we have developed and kept faith in the jury system. This is based on the view that regular people are able to make decisions about complex problems and that the integrity and lack of vested interests of those involved is more important than the experience of members of an establishment.

In a jury system lay people are selected to come to a decision on behalf of the community, choosing between two competing arguments. People in juries are trusted to make decisions which can have profound impacts on people's lives and there is no reason why similar people cannot choose between political alternatives.

The philosophy of the "wisdom of crowds" also demonstrates that a group of people can usually find a remarkably accurate solution to a problem through combining their independent assessments. It is known as "common sense".

The concept of proper representation of the community is at the core of the proposals by the Jury Team which links this basic concept of fairness with a practical way of achieving significant change through the established UK constitution. In the same way that jurors are selected from their community to decide cases, elected representatives can be drawn from a much wider and yet more local group than is the current case with career MEP/MPs.

The Jury Team therefore proposes a radical change in the way in which MEP/MPs are selected so that, in the same way as a jury, they can go back to being independent people exercising their best judgment and not just delegates of a political party leadership. Gilbert and Sullivan described this need in their 1875 *Trial by Jury:*

Now, Jurymen, hear my advice--
All kinds of vulgar prejudice
I pray you set aside:
With stern, judicial frame of mind
From bias free of every kind,
This trial must be tried.

The End Of The Party

Proposal and Handbook

By The

JURY TEAM

Jury Team is a registered political party

All enquiries:

www.juryteam.org

ISBN Number 978-0-9561964-0-8

British Library Cataloguing in Publication Data.
A catalogue record for this book is available from the British Library.

Printed in England by imprintdigital.net

First Published March 2009

Contents

The Jury Team Principles

Government should be run for the benefit of the people and not for the benefit of any political party.

Elected representatives should vote according to their view of what is best for the country and their constituents and not at the direction of a political party.

Politicians should fully comply with the Nolan Principles of Public Life and have externally decided and transparent remuneration.

Politics for the People

Politics without Parties

Politics with Principles

This Proposal and Handbook is designed for everyone involved with the Jury Team, especially its candidates and members. It describes the key features of its Principles and Proposals and the current practical and governance issues affecting the United Kingdom. Suggestions for further reading are shown in Appendix 1.

Proposal

Chapter 1

INTRODUCTION AND SUMMARY

"The old order changeth, giving way to new."
~ Tennyson

"If the turkeys won't vote for our Christmas, we need to change the turkeys."

1. Preface

The Jury Team, launched in mid March 2009, was founded for those people who believe in democracy but who have observed how the current party political system has turned the United Kingdom's Parliament and Government into the creatures of a small and increasingly distant group of oligarchical politicians.

The arrogance that has developed in these party cultures has led to personal behaviours and attitudes on issues such as expenses and conflicts of interest which would be unacceptable in any other walk of life. Politicians are seen as more interested in winning elections than in improving the lot of the people or the state of the nation. Many manipulate rather than respect their electorate. MPs are now largely in Parliament as their primary career rather than to provide objective oversight of the Government.

The party whipping system has generally reduced the House of Commons to a talking shop which overwhelmingly accepts the Government's proposals with little scrutiny. The UK Government is run by ministers appointed for party political reasons who have little background in their subject or in management and are anyway moved elsewhere before they can implement their proposals. Similar issues exist in the European Parliament and in other EU institutions.

These problems are linked by the common thread of the self-destructing nature of party politics and have been identified previously by many observers. This document brings them together to provide all those who want to work towards change with the necessary information about how they can make a difference.

This is however not simply a work of analysis. The distinguishing feature of an entrepreneur is that he or she does not just have a good idea but also expends effort in actually implementing it. This Proposal and Handbook therefore not only sets out the key issues facing the UK and its governance. It also shows how by using modern technology we can now restore proper democracy and integrity to our democratic institutions by allowing people, selected openly by their fellow citizens, to become independent MPs and MEPs.

The Jury Team is organising a nationally coordinated process through its website *www.juryteam.org* to select its candidates, using mobile phone technology, in the equivalent of a primary election. It will then support the election of the chosen Jury Team candidates to become independent MPs and MEPs. When elected they will not be subject to a party whip but will all be committed to improving the governance of Parliaments and Governments.

Jury Team candidates will be selected as potential MEPs for the 2009 European Parliament elections on the 4th June 2009, as potential MPs for whenever the next general election is held in 2009/10 and for the 2011 Scotland, Wales, Northern Ireland and Local Government elections.

The Jury Team will work within the established constitution which however, without asking the people, has been changed over the last two centuries to give a concentration of power to self-serving political parties. This has led to institutional corruption as the original checks and balances have been eroded. In this respect the Jury Team has the same approach as did Martin Luther to the church of the 15th Century. He revered the ecclesiastical philosophy but was determined to remove what he saw as the modern corruptions of what had once been a noble calling.

2. The Consequences of our Party Political System

The strident party political nature of modern UK politics has led to the country facing serious problems. The unchecked and unscrutinised concentration of party political power results in the party benefit outweighing the national benefit when decisions are made in areas such as:

- approval of legislation
- taxation, spending and investment
- public services such as health, education and transport
- departmental announcements and use of statistics
- regulation and enforcement
- appointments

Decisions made by politicians with their eye constantly on their electoral prospects now lead to the party leaders offering continual verbal bribes to the electorate in the same way as Roman emperors used to try to stay in power by offering "bread and circuses" to their citizens.

Lord (Robin) Butler, who served as Cabinet Secretary from 1988 to 1998 with Margaret Thatcher, John Major and Tony Blair, and who therefore observed the process as closely as anyone, stated in a 2004 interview in The Spectator:

"I think we are a country where we suffer very badly from Parliament not having sufficient control over the executive and that is a very grave flaw. We should be breaking away from the party whip. The executive is much too free to bring in a huge number of extremely bad Bills, a huge amount of regulation and to do whatever it likes — and whatever it likes is what will get the best headlines tomorrow. All that is part of what is bad Government in this country."

Political parties have grown during the last two centuries until they now have a stranglehold not only on the selection of Members of Parliament but also through the whipping system on the way in which they must vote once elected. Career MPs become chained to the platform of their chosen party for their advancement. The biographies of many of the front bench members of the main political parties are almost indistinguishable on their well-trodden path from college to party worker to Whitehall. Their entire working life requires obedience to their party leadership who promulgate changing policies of which they may only agree with a few.

Our "first past the post" (FPTP) Westminster election system inevitably leads to the dominance of an oligarchy of only two major parties in which an increasingly small number of individuals have the media access to dominate politics. The legislature, our Parliament, and the executive, our Government, have now merged under the Prime Minister who commands his or her majority in Parliament though the whips and the administration of existing laws though the ministers. His or her appointments of both whips and ministers are made in the interests of the governing party and not of the people of the United Kingdom. There are no proper checks and balances against the actions of these appointees either in Parliament or in the major departments of state.

In the *Palgrave Macmillan Dictionary of Political Thought*, Roger Scruton defines the Political Class as: *"The class, increasingly important in modern democratic politics, of people who have made a career in political and administrative institutions, but who have not had any experience of the ordinary workplace."*

Peter Oborne, the experienced political journalist, says in his book *The Triumph of the Political Class*:

> *"The Political Class has come to acquire one of the defining characteristics of a social class: a common economic base. Politicians are now fundamentally dependent for funding and prestige upon the British state. Indeed many members of the Political Class abuse their financial and other privileges, then collaborate with each other, even across traditional party lines, to prevent themselves being found out.*

The techniques of manipulation, deception, smear and institutional capture have taken power away from ordinary voters and placed it in the hands of the Political Class. But this means that democratic politics in Britain no longer does the job most people want it to do. Rather than resolve conflict, it suppresses it. Rather than inform voters, it deceives them. Rather than place a check on the power of the executive, it celebrates it. This is a fantastically dangerous structure.

Voters put their MPs into parliament to represent their interests, and to articulate their anger, not to form part of a comfortable club, or to collude with opposition parties"

The search for a stance and image which will lead to a political party being elected, requiring it to move towards the centre, means that all major parties have to have policies which pander to and do not upset the floating voters.

It is for instance now clear that the economic growth of the last 15 years has been built on too much debt. However because they needed to compete in the minds of voters to say that they could improve living standards, no major party proposed any measures to restrict banks and building societies from providing loans and other credit instruments, such as 125% mortgages, which clearly could not be sustainable.

Sir Ken Macdonald, Director of Public Prosecutions from 2003-08, wrote in The Times in February 2009:

"How did we get here? Well, financial deregulation undoubtedly released great energy and wealth into the markets and did so in part by giving bankers and financiers more space. But this space had another effect. It created a growing distance between wealthy and powerful individuals and the agencies designed to police their behaviour.

Not sensing the danger in this, our two main political parties supported looser regulation over many years. Now, apparently tainted by past misjudgments, they are deeply compromised in trying to find solutions."

Governments based on political parties inevitably choose the soft option for the floating voters, whether in relation to infrastructure, pensions, education or health. In contrast, it is most unlikely that independent MPs would have voted for the Iraq War, for identity cards or for many of the more than one thousand new criminal offences which have been enacted in the past decade.

The End Of The Party

In the last 35 years since 1974, the UK has had six Prime Ministers. Labour held power from 1974 to 1979 (Wilson and Callaghan), the Conservatives from 1979 to 1997 (Thatcher and Major) and New Labour from 1997 to probably 2010 (Blair and Brown). In each case the Prime Minister elected at the beginning of the Government resigned under a serious cloud and the successor, not elected by the voters, lost (or in the case of Brown may well lose) a general election. These six people came from very different backgrounds with markedly diverse political philosophies and personal character traits but none of them has been able effectively to run the current system of political parties and Government for the long-term benefit of the country and its people.

The inevitable conclusion of these more than three decades of political frustration is that it is very unlikely that whoever is elected at the next general election will be able to deal with the key issues facing the country within the current "yah-boo" party political system. Given the huge ramifications for millions of people it is clearly not sensible just to wait for a "Master or Mistress of the Universe" to appear who can operate this system effectively. A better approach must be to review what is wrong with the current party political system and to see how it can be improved so that the issues facing voters can be better resolved.

In an Editorial in November 2008, The Times said:

> *"Britain has more children leaving school at 16 than any comparable nation. A tiny fraction of crimes are seen all the way through to prosecution. The incapacity benefit bill is still huge. So are the unfunded pensions liabilities. There has been a decade-long experiment in the social democratic idea that money and a modicum of efficiency saving will lead to drastic improvement. It has failed to do so and there is now no option other than fundamental reform of the State."*

A review of the national issues facing the UK is in Chapter 2A.

The public is also very concerned about the backgrounds, lifestyles and expenses of MPs, exemplified by issues such as the John Lewis list. On the 3rd July 2008, MPs threw out a series of proposed reforms to their expenses by 172 to 144. This not only prevented the necessary reforms but showed that 325, over half, of the eligible 641 MPs (excluding the Speaker and four tellers) actually failed to vote. The abstentions were made up 42% of all Labour MPs, 43% of all Liberal Democrats, 61% of all Conservatives and 83% of all the other parties.

The Jury Team will therefore have three over-riding principles:

- **Government should be run for the benefit of the people and not for the benefit of any political party.**

- **Elected representatives should vote according to their view of what is best for the country and their constituents and not at the direction of a political party.**

- **Politicians should fully comply with the Nolan Principles of Public Life and have externally decided and transparent remuneration.**

3. <u>Trust in Parliament and Government</u>

The UK political system has lost the respect of its citizens. This is evidenced by:

- the low turnout at elections:

    - only two-fifths of registered electors voted at both of the 2001 and 2005 general elections and only three-fifths of registered electors voted at each

    - only two-fifths of registered electors voted at the 2004 European Parliamentary election, which was combined with the local elections, and less than a quarter voted at the previous 1999 European Parliamentary election

- continuing criticism of MPs' lifestyles, of Government initiatives and of the delivery of public services (MPs and ministers are trusted by only 27% and 24% of citizens respectively)

The particularly serious issues with the UK party political system are confirmed by the latest *Eurobarometer* survey published by the European Commission in June 2008. This was based on over 30,000 interviews across the EU with a minimum of 1,000 interviewees in each country, including 1,306 in the UK. One of the sections was: *"I would like to ask you a question about how much trust you have in certain institutions. For each of the following institutions, please tell me if you tend to trust it or tend not to trust it."*

The results of the survey fully support the thesis of the Jury Team. Only 27% of UK citizens said that they trusted the UK Parliament and only 24% said that they trusted the UK Government. This result was the lowest of any part of the EU and demonstrates that the UK electorate has come to a much deeper suspicion about its political system than exists in other broadly comparable countries. This is a very sad position and should be a wake-up call for all of those who believe that the UK deserves a better system of Government and that the *"Mother of Parliaments"* should be reformed in order to gain greater respect:

Tend to trust the National Parliament		Tend to trust the National Government	
Denmark	76%	Finland	61%
Finland	66%	Malta	56%
Sweden	60%	Spain	55%
Netherlands	56%	Denmark	55%
Spain	54%	Netherlands	51%
Malta	54%	Sweden	45%
Greece	49%	Austria	42%
Belgium	48%	Belgium	40%
Austria	46%	Ireland	37%
Ireland	42%	Germany	36%
Germany	41%	Greece	34%
Portugal	39%	Portugal	32%
France	35%	France	28%
UK	**27%**	**UK**	**24%**

65% of the UK respondents specifically said that they did not trust Parliament and 72% said they did not trust the Government.

Similarly UK surveys in 2000 and 2004 showed that 54% and 55% of voters thought that *"this country is getting less democratic"* with only 22% and 24% having the opposite view.

63% of people polled in 2004 said they thought *"the present system of governing Britain" "could be improved quite a lot"* or *"needs a great deal of improvement".*

Further information about how our Parliament and Government have evolved is described in Chapter 2B.

Despite the issues in Parliament and Government, the UK has a very well developed civil society. This is especially so in the charitable sector where 170,000 organisations, with a total income of £46 billion, have over half a million paid staff and millions of volunteers supporting them. Some, such as the National Trust, have memberships many times greater than all political parties combined. They also have a strong tradition of independence and integrity which contrasts greatly with the image of Parliament and Government. The experience of our civil society can undoubtedly contribute to reforming our key political institutions and to providing Jury Team Parliamentary candidates.

4. <u>Survey Evidence</u>

The Jury Team organized a national survey to determine voter attitudes. All figures are from YouGov Plc which conducted the poll. YouGov is a member of the British Polling Council and is registered with the Information Commissioner. The total sample size was 2161 adults. Fieldwork was undertaken between the 30th January and 2nd February 2009. The survey was carried out online. The figures have been weighted and are representative of all GB adults (aged 18+).

The questions asked are shown in italics below followed by the responses.

a. The public graphically demonstrated that they believe that politicians currently act overwhelmingly in the interests of their political party and themselves rather than of the country or their constituents:

When acting in a political capacity which ONE of the following BEST describes whose interests you think politicians generally put first?

	Total	Male	Female
Their party's	**44%**	42%	45%
Their own	**42%**	44%	41%
The country's	8%	8%	8%
Their constituents'	5%	5%	4%
Other	2%	1%	2%

44% of all respondents therefore stated that politicians generally put their party's interests first. 86% of all respondents, and of both male and female respondents, stated that politicians generally put either their party's or their own interests first. Only 13% of respondents stated that politicians generally put first the interest of the country (8%) or their constituents (5%).

b. The public fully understand the need to make government more accountable:

Below are some areas that could be priorities for politicians to have. It is not a full list but please select up to 3 options from those shown which you would like to be your elected representative's main priorities.

	Total	Male	Female
Strengthening the economy	71%	70%	72%
Reducing crime and vandalism	66%	67%	66%
Improving the management of immigration	53%	51%	55%
Making government more accountable	**42%**	46%	37%
Investing in public services	38%	38%	39%
Enhancing Britain's diplomatic standing in the world	7%	8%	6%
Other	3%	3%	3%
Don't know	3%	2%	4%

Over two-fifths of people (42%) rated "Making government more accountable" as one of their top three issues. This was higher than the 38% who stated "Investing in public services" as one of their top three issues.

5. Recent Quotations

In his speech at the Haltemprice & Howden by-election in July 2008, Bob Geldof identified that Parliament is no longer standing up to the executive:

"Let us be grand for once then, for we talk of great subjects. Let us ask 'what is the point of England' now that Parliament, whose primary purpose is to defend the liberties of the people, have so gratuitously, so wantonly, so casually betrayed that trust and taken from us that same liberty which above all else defines this country and its constitution, and that which has been its greatest gift to the world: its freedom, its tolerances, its civilisation which William Wilberforce so forcefully argued from this town so many centuries ago."

At an October 2008 conference, Martin Bell, the former Independent MP, spoke about the growing need for people who are free of political sway, and *"only want to serve the people who voted them in"*. He said:

"Negative 'Punch and Judy' politics are not working anymore. Independents practice a different kind of politics, gentler and closer to the people, and we need that now more than ever before."

Professor Anthony King, the political scientist, wrote in the Daily Telegraph in December 2008:

"However, the truth is that the deepest divide in British politics today is not between Labour and the Tories; or between Speaker Michael Martin and irate backbench MPs; or between members of Gordon Brown's Cabinet and each other. It is between Britain's whole political class and the great majority of the British people. On the far side of a chasm stand politicians of all parties and their hangers-on. On the near side is almost everyone else.

Part of the answer lies in a crucial fact that almost everyone in Britain is dimly aware of but that has yet to find full expression. It is that our system of government is failing to perform adequately.

The End Of The Party

Governments of both major parties blunder and fail far more often than they used to.

The past three decades have given us the BSE debacle; the poll tax; the Child Support Agency; Britain's ignominious expulsion from the European Exchange Rate Mechanism; the Millennium Dome; the massive cost-overruns and the partial or total failure of IT projects across the public sector; the failure to control immigration; the bungled introduction of home information packs (Hips); the abandonment of supercasinos; the fiasco of the cost-ineffective Assets Recovery Agency; the collapse of Metronet; GPs' and dentists' ill-drafted contracts; Northern Rock; the failure of government regulation across the financial sector; the botched marking of last summer's SATS exams; the mishandling of Post Office card accounts; the shambolic arrest of Damian Green, and a great deal else besides. And we still have ID cards and the London Olympics to look forward to."

In a December 2008 debate in the House of Lords, the Conservative peer Lord Norton of Louth, Chair of the Lords Constitution Select Committee from 2001-04, stated:

"There are significant changes in the very nature of politics. Some people are losing interest in politics; others are not losing interest but rather diverting their attention away from political parties to interest groups. There has been a phenomenal growth in the number of interest groups over the past 40 years. The membership of political parties has seen a major decline as the membership of interest groups has increased. We need to be in a position to engage both with those who come together to form particular groups and those individuals who believe that politics, and what Parliament does, is not for them. There have also been major changes in the means available for communication, especially electronic means."

In the light of the unprecedented issues in the financial markets and increasingly in the rest of the economy, Frank Field, the Labour MP, wrote in the Guardian in December 2008 that we now need to start preparing for a national Government:

"If the Government fails to survive the economic catastrophe beginning to engulf practically all of us, its inability to finance record-breaking debt is what will probably bring it down. Any such

end is likely to come unexpectedly, so we need to start planning what to do.

If the debt can't be sold, it will be impossible for the Government to continue. The only options then will be to print money, with all the dangers for a country of going along with such a policy; or for the political parties to come together - in a national Government - to try to convince the gilt market that the country is serious about bringing under control the gap between projected Government expenditure and its falling tax revenue base.

It is crucial that we begin to plan for this scenario for, once in this totally uncharted territory, we may not then have that long to convince the markets that Britain's political class really means business in trying to get the nation's accounts into some sort of order. If we fail to convince at this point, then the outlook for the country is truly unimaginable."

In a December 2008 article in the Mail on Sunday, Vince Cable, the Liberal Democrat MP and Treasury Spokesman, wrote:

"I believe the public will see the need to 'stick together' and, in particular, will expect the political parties to rise above the usual petty, tribal bickering. There will be calls for a 'government of national unity', to get political adversaries round a table working together rather than pointing fingers at each other. There must, of course, be vigorous debate and public accountability, as well as unity, but I think the public senses that this is not what they are getting at the moment.

I see the personal and party animosities played out every week at Westminster and wonder if the political classes are capable of grasping the enormity of the crisis we are in and the challenge to us to behave differently. If we do not, the public will become seriously angry. We know from history that such anger can lead to extremes.

It will no longer be acceptable for Ministers and mandarins (or MPs and peers) to have a feather-bedded existence, with large, protected pension pots, like First World War generals enjoying the comforts of a chateau at the rear while their men are fighting in the trenches."

6. The Party Political System and Elections

Political parties require loyalty to their leadership which is completely alien to the proper role of a democratic politician's key responsibility to his or her constituents or to the country as a whole. Political parties are now seen as being more concerned with winning elections than with actually improving the lives of the people they represent. The key objective of modern political parties is to gain and keep power for themselves rather than to run the Government for the benefit of the people or to ensure that Government is properly scrutinised by Parliament.

For 500 years after Magna Carta, Parliament had no political parties. Each MP voted according to their own conscience. Even during the 19th Century, many of the most important initiatives, such as the abolition of the slave trade or the development of the railway system, were the result of private members' bills. However as the electoral franchise was extended, and the secret ballot introduced, the central party political organisations became more powerful and now dominate elections and the conduct and voting of MPs.

Graham Allen, the Labour MP, says in his book *The Last Prime Minister*:

> *"Political legitimacy became synonymous with directly elected representation and as the franchise got wider electoral legitimacy was monopolised by the Commons, who in order to execute their parties' objectives, in turn ceded their political sovereignty to their leaderships. The more the MP's electability depended upon the public perception of the Prime Minister, the more exclusive became his power. Thus was completed the vacuous circle which characterizes British politics today."*

The active membership of political parties has dropped to less than 1% of the UK population. In many parts of the UK the Labour or Conservative parties no longer have any effective local representation. Party members are much older than the electorate in total and they are atypical on a number of other measures. The great majority of MPs have had little association with their constituencies before they were elected.

The End Of The Party

For Westminster elections, over three quarters of Parliamentary seats are safe under any likely political balance between the two main parties. The FPTP electoral system therefore results in most votes not counting. This means that the political parties only have to concentrate on the 20% of seats, about 130, which are likely to change hands. Within these seats only about 10% of the electorate are targetable floating voters and therefore all of the campaigning is concentrated on the 10% of 20%, being 2%, of the 45 million registered voters. These 900,000 people have their views carefully canvassed and are the focus of all of the centrally directed campaign activity.

Three fifths of the public no longer perceive that the main political parties have any substantially different policies and they feel that political debate is shallow. The two main parties adjust their policies, candidates and leaders to try to win the election by influencing the 900,000 floating voters.

For instance, Stephen Byers, the former Labour minister, wrote in The Sunday Times in May 2008:

> *"In the past year far too many decisions about tax have been taken to try to secure a tactical advantage. This has led to some damaging mistakes. Whether in relation to the changes to inheritance tax, capital gains tax, the treatment of non-doms or the abolition of the 10p income tax band, the whole approach has been about political positioning. What has been lacking is a strategic and principled view of how we should change our tax regime."*

Turnout decreased to around 60% in the 2001 and 2005 general elections. The 40% abstaining therefore form the largest voting group. Governments have been put in power by a decreasing share of the votes of the total electorate: from 33.5% in 1992, to 30.9% in 1987, to 24.8% in 2001 and to only 21.6% in 2005. The current Government's legitimacy is therefore based on the endorsement of only slightly more than a fifth of the electorate.

General elections using the FPTP system lead to substantial differences between the share of votes and seats and therefore do not lead to a Parliament reflecting the will of the people. Major parties normally do better in terms of seats and minor parties worse. Similarly there are geographical distortions with, for example, the largest number of voters in England supporting the Conservative Party in 2005 but with Labour getting 90 more English seats.

Parliament also does not represent the population proportionately. Compared with their share of the population, women currently have only about 40% of their proper representation as MPs and ethnic minorities only about 30%.

More background about the issues surrounding political parties and elections is provided in Chapter 2C.

The Jury Team seeks the election of independent MPs. These will better tend to reflect the electorate and to have a close relationship with their local community with their attitudes being more likely to be compatible with their electorate because of the way in which they have been chosen.

7. Voter Volatility

The low membership of political parties and declining turnout at elections shows voters' distaste for the existing way of doing politics. They have reduced party allegiance and express the wish to have politicians who do not have the prejudices and arrogance of political parties.

As it champions the key integrity issues important to the British people, the Jury Team has the opportunity to get back into the political system the majority of the electorate who do not usually vote as they have previously seen little benefit in doing so because of the entrenched party systems. It can also attract those who have supported the traditional parties but have become distanced from their antics. A 2005 YouGov poll showed that 24% of the electorate would vote for "none of the above" without even knowing what might be the alternatives. The Jury Team may even entice some of the estimated 7% of eligible adults who are not currently signed up to vote to become registered electors in a similar way to what happened in the US with Barack Obama.

Political loyalties which used to be handed down from generation to generation are no longer strong. Society has changed as citizens have become much more aware than a few decades ago of the complexity of life and of political issues.

The reasons for this reduction in political allegiance include better education and more travel, the lessening importance of family networks, fewer locational ties, the reduction in class-based inequalities and greater suspicion of politicians themselves. People have a wide range of views and will not slavishly follow the policies of one political party.

There has been a particular reduction in interest by young people who have generally grown up in better conditions than previous generations. Although around three-quarters of them are interested in political issues, only two-fifths have any interest in party politics.

40 years ago over 90% of the electorate had a clear preference for a political party and over 40% identified strongly with one. Nowadays only 10% of the electorate strongly identifies with any political party: 90% of the electorate is open to hear arguments about which party they should support.

Voters are therefore not at all wedded to the traditional parties. In the 2005 general election less than half of people thought that any political party properly represented their views. 59% of the electorate either voted for a party that was neither the Conservatives nor Labour or did not vote at all. Similarly there were 311 of the 646 constituencies where parties other than Labour or the Conservatives were in first or second place.

Many voters also change their minds between elections. In the 2005 general election only 38% of registered voters voted for the same party as they did in 2001. 21% did not vote at either election. The other 41% were made up of 19% who only voted at one of the elections, 14% who switched votes and 7% who were new voters.

There is also substantial volatility during the campaign itself. In 2005 only 35% of the electorate voted as they said they would at the beginning of the campaign, the other 65% either not voting or changing their allegiance. Indeed a 2005 survey by MORI showed that over a quarter of voters were undecided on the day immediately before the election.

There is therefore no doubt that the modern UK population is amenable to changing its voting patterns. Further background to this is shown in Chapter 2D.

8. Campaigning

In the Introduction to his book *How to win Campaigns,* Chris Rose, who has worked for Greenpeace, Friends of the Earth, and WWF International, states:

> *Campaigning is an expression of popular democracy; it creates new channels of influence for the public in the public interest. Campaigns work in the public interest by borrowing power from the people for good causes. In a world where politics are increasingly professionalized and lean increasingly towards promotion of private economic interests, campaigning has often become the common politics of the people.*

He describes some of the reasons why campaigning works:

- *It creates gearing – multiplies the impact of efforts at change by enlisting the help of many people, thereby making it possible to achieve particular changes more quickly, or bigger changes altogether*

- *It sets agendas – it aligns the public about what needs to be done*

- *It can remedy a democratic deficit, compensating for the corporatisation and professionalisation of politics and the consequent spiraling lack of trust in the formal political system*

- *For the time being, NGOs – and this includes many campaign groups – are generally more trusted than most other elements of society, such as businesses, politicians and paid-for scientists*

- *It creates a community and ecology of action – it means people are 'not alone'.*

9. The Benefit of Juries

Bill Cash, the Conservative MP, wrote in October 2008 about the 150th anniversary of the launch by John Bright of his historic campaign for working men to get the vote. Cash said:

"Bright, with Richard Cobden, his fellow believer in free trade, had in 1846 saved the masses from starvation by forcing Peel to repeal the Corn Laws.

So if Bright were alive today what would he be fighting for? His absolute priority would be to restore respect and authority to the Commons. The man who coined the phrase "the Mother of Parliaments" believed that the most precious thing that a person possessed was the right to vote for the laws that governed him and his country.

Bright's first allegiance was to his conscience. He would have no truck with the modern whips system and the surrender of parliamentary business to the executive, nor the fixing of timetables to prevent debate - such as the mere nine minutes given to the third reading of the Embryology Bill last week."

Through the last eight centuries we have developed and kept faith in the jury system. This is based on the view that regular people are able to make decisions about complex problems and that the integrity and lack of vested interests of those involved is more important than the experience of members of an establishment.

In a jury system lay people are selected to come to a decision on behalf of the community, choosing between two competing arguments. People in juries are trusted to make decisions which can have profound impacts on people's lives and there is no reason why similar people cannot choose between political alternatives.

The philosophy of the "wisdom of crowds" also demonstrates that a group of people can usually find a remarkably accurate solution to a problem through combining their independent assessments. It is known as "common sense".

The concept of proper representation of the community is at the core of the proposals by the Jury Team which link this basic concept of fairness with a practical way of achieving significant change through the established UK constitution. In the same way that jurors are selected from their communities to decide cases, MPs can be drawn from a much wider and yet more local group than is the current case with career MEP/MPs.

There are those such as the author Keith Sutherland who believe that we would be best served if Parliament was also filled, like a jury, on an entirely random basis. However those who propose this recognise that it cannot be achieved within the constitution.

The Jury Team therefore proposes a radical change in the way in which MEP/MPs are selected so that, in the same way as a jury, they can go back to being independent people exercising their best judgment and not just delegates of a political party leadership. Gilbert and Sullivan described this need in their 1875 *Trial by Jury:*

Now, Jurymen, hear my advice--
All kinds of vulgar prejudice
I pray you set aside:
With stern, judicial frame of mind
From bias free of every kind,
This trial must be tried.

CHORUS

From bias free of every kind,
This trial must be tried.

10. The Need for the Right People and Structures

The world changes so quickly that no party political manifesto can hope to cover all of the issues which are likely to arise even in the term of a five year Government. Indeed it is clear that most votes are anyway cast in a general election by people who have not read the main party manifestos and have only a very limited knowledge of their contents. The claim of a political party to have a mandate for each of its policy proposals is therefore of little merit.

Anatole Kaletsky wrote in The Times in August 2008:

The End Of The Party

"Manifestos are rarely worth the paper they are written on. This is not just because politicians are dishonest but because unexpected events intervene. Dealing with the unexpected is a much more important function of government than implementing manifestos."

In order to be able to lead and/or manage any organisation it is first necessary to get right both the people and the structures in which they operate. Properly qualified people must be in place and able to use their best unbiased judgment in deciding how to progress all of the issues which do arise. They need to do this in organisational structures which encourage sensible debate and decision making. Only when these two elements are in place is it likely that there will be any proper, reasonable and judicious discussion about the particular way forward.

This principle is well described by Professor Jim Collins in his seminal book on leadership, *From Good to Great*, in which he describes his concept of "First Who, Then What". The main point of this is not just about assembling the right team. The key is to get the right people on the bus (and the wrong people off the bus) before you decide where and how to drive it. He says:

- First Who: Get the right people on the bus. Build a superior team

- Then What: Once you have the right people in place, figure out the best path

The Jury Team therefore deliberately does not address itself to policies on specific issues relating to the economy, public services or other aspects of Government activity. The Jury Team believes that these are up to the judgment of those who are elected. The Jury Team process of openly selecting its candidates is much more likely to reflect the will of the people of the UK.

Further details about the Jury Team are in Chapter 3.

As well as having the right people it is also necessary to have the right structures in which they operate.

Unfortunately the UK governance structures have become dominated by party politics and by the merger for all practical purposes of Parliament and Government. Parliament has lost its powers properly to scrutinise proposed legislation and to review the decisions of the Government. The central Government machine has changed little in structure for over 150 years despite the massive increases in its scope. The leadership of the departments is by politicians with short-term political aspirations, minimal management experience and fast career changes who generate initiatives more for media consumption than for the benefit of the public.

A failure to reform the governance structures will condemn the UK to the continuing failure of so many of its government related activities as outlined above.

The Jury Team therefore believes that as well as getting properly independent people into Parliament it is essential for the future development and success of the UK that its national governance structures are substantially improved.

11. Improving Governance

Whatever their political views, all Jury Team candidates will have to commit to improving the governance of Parliament and Government. The first key element of this is that all Jury Team candidates will agree to remaining independent.

In addition the Jury Team has researched a wide range of sources which over the last few years have looked at the governance of the UK including:

- Electoral Reform Society
- Hansard Society
- Power Inquiry
- Better Government Initiative
- Democratic Audit
- Unlock Democracy/ Charter 88
- Open Democracy/ Our Kingdom
- Electoral Commission
- Committee on Standards in Public Life (Nolan)
- Commons Home Affairs Select Committee

- Commons Public Administration Select Committee
- Lords Constitution Select Committee
- Hayden Phillips Report on Party Funding

In addition the results of many public opinion polls have been reviewed to determine the governance issues which most concern the electorate.

These reviews were collated to produce the three Jury Team Governance Principles set out above in Chapter 1.2. They have been developed into twelve specific Jury Team Governance Proposals which are designed to clean up UK politics and provide a proper framework for political activity. These describe a potential framework for new House of Commons Standing Orders and for the legislative programme in the Queen's Speech which opens the first Parliament after the next general election.

As they are independent, candidates for the Jury Team will not be required to accept in detail all of the elements of the twelve Governance Proposals, but will confirm in their application that they *"support the three Jury Team Principles and all policies which lead to better governance of parliament and government."* They will therefore be committed to introducing legislation, such as in the Governance Proposals, to ensure that the political system meets the ethical, effectiveness, efficiency and economic criteria which are expected in all other walks of British life. They will be able to state on their application form their views on the Governance Proposals so that those members of the public selecting them have this information.

The detail of the Jury Team Governance Proposals will be reviewed in the new Westminster and European Parliaments to ensure that they are robust and that all of the consequential details have been accounted for.

The key elements of the Proposals are:

- The UK Parliament will again be made free to critique UK and European legislation
- All MPs and MEPs will have to accept normal salary, expense and pension conditions and a limit on the time they serve as

MPs and to keep to the Nolan Principles of Selflessness, Integrity, Objectivity, Accountability, Openness, Honesty and Leadership.

- An independent Politicians Complaints Commission will be set up to look at all alleged conflicts of interest and transgressions by Ministers, MPs, Lords and UK MEPs

- The funding of political parties will be legitimised

- General elections will be held every five years, rather than at a time of the Prime Minister's choosing, unless the House of Commons votes to shorten this period because of particular circumstances

- People will be able to call for a UK referendum on all appropriate issues in order to provide a further check on Government (a proposal supported by 70% of the public)

- The management and administration of Government departments will be improved by introducing independent scrutiny and by insisting that all national statistics are prepared and presented independently of Government.

The 12 statements in the Jury Team Governance Proposals are set out at the end of this Chapter and their rationale is described in the Governance Section of this Handbook.

12. <u>The Process for Nominating Jury Team Candidates</u>

The Jury Team has registered the website *www.juryteam.org*. This web presence will be a central part of the selection and election process, releasing the energy and involvement of the electorate in the same way as achieved by Barack Obama in the US. The site will include sections on all of those standing to be selected and then elected, on the latest news affecting UK and EU politics, and on ways in which the public can volunteer to help and donate.

The website will provide a fresh start for UK politics by allowing people to put themselves up for selection as a candidate for the Jury Team in the same way as happens for primary elections in the US.

This will break the oligopoly of the three main existing parties who have an iron grip on the selection of potential MPs and MEPs. These parties only generally allow candidates who have been approved through a central, and secretive, system to stand for selection by individual constituency associations who anyway do not properly represent the electorate.

The Conservative MP, Douglas Carswell, wrote in the March 2009 edition of the magazine TotalPolitics:

"I believe that we need a system of open primary selection to decide who stands for Parliament. Open primaries would allow outsiders and those without the backing of the party machine to have a place in politics."

The *www.juryteam.org* website will make it possible for anyone who wants to stand as a candidate for the Jury Team to do so very easily. There will be an on-line form to complete, as shown in Appendix 2 for the Westminster Parliament, and the details on this will then be available for all to see on the website.

It is expected that candidates will have a wide range of backgrounds from the private, charity and public sectors. They are likely to be very largely local with a traditional commitment to their region or constituency unlike the majority of current MPs.

This opening up of political campaigning was described in an August 2008 report *The Future of Politics* by Orange, in association with The Future Laboratory. It states:

"The 2008 US presidential campaign has already demonstrated the power the internet brings to political campaigning.

Perhaps the greatest benefit of the internet is that it lowers the barriers to entry into political campaigning. Citizens no longer need to be part of a political party to lend their ideas and organising skills."

13. Selection of Candidates

The selection of the candidates to stand for the Jury Team is equivalent to the process of primaries in choosing a Congressional or Presidential candidate in the US. The essential feature of a primary is that all adults are entitled to vote, not just the paid up members of the political parties. The Jury Team will have a similar open process in the UK.

People have become used to making selections in other fields, such as television shows, with their computer and mobile phone. The technology used by the Jury Team combines the use of a computer with a mobile phone to ensure maximum accuracy and security.

According to Ofcom, in 2008 there were 123 active mobile phone connections for every 100 people. 92% of households have a mobile phone. This therefore gives a vastly greater coverage of those able to select their candidate than has been possible with the traditional political parties in their selection meetings in "church halls" where only a small number of people, normally atypical of the population, are present.

Existing MEPs and MPs will be invited to become Jury Team candidates if they leave their party and accept the three Jury Team Governance Principles. They will usually stand in their existing region or constituency.

14. Election of Candidates

Once the Jury Team candidates have been selected by the public's mobile phone voting then the Jury Team will put all of its efforts into getting those candidates elected. The candidates will stand in the actual elections against the candidates of the traditional parties and will be shown on the ballot paper as Jury Team candidates.

In the YouGov poll described in Section 4 above, the Jury Team also asked questions about people's attitudes to voting for independent candidates.

a. People responded that they mainly did not vote for independent candidates because they did not think they would win rather than because the person was wedded to a particular party. This gives a tremendous opportunity for the Jury Team to demonstrate its credibility and its potential influence:

Thinking about times you have voted in general elections, if you have generally not voted for independent candidates which (if any) of the following is the MAIN reason for this?

	Total	Male	Female
They stand little chance of being elected	**21%**	20%	21%
Elected councillors and other politicians can seldom achieve anything unless they are part of a bigger group or party	**12%**	13%	11%
They are unlikely to become part of the Government	**10%**	11%	10%
I have never had the opportunity to vote for an independent candidate	**10%**	11%	9%
I actively support an established political party	10%	11%	9%

43% of people (the first three categories) therefore generally have not voted for an independent candidate because they feel they are unlikely to succeed or to form the government. A further 10% have not had the opportunity to vote for an independent candidate, to give a total of 53%.

Only 10% would not vote for an independent candidate because they "actively support a political party".

The position is remarkably similar for male and female voters.

b. The opportunity for Jury Team candidates is shown clearly by the response to a question asking if people would vote for a credible independent candidate.

I would consider voting for an Independent candidate if they stood a reasonably good chance of being elected.

	Total	Male	Female
Strongly agree	**17%**	19%	15%
Agree	**38%**	38%	38%
Neither agree nor disagree	21%	19%	22%
Disagree	13%	14%	13%
Strongly disagree	6%	8%	4%
Don't know	6%	4%	8%

55% of people agree with the statement (17% strongly agree and 38% agree). Only 19% disagree. This shows the potential of the Jury Team. The 55% figure is similar to the 60%/58%/58% support achieved by independents Martin Bell, Richard Taylor and Peter Law at the 1997, 2001 and 2005 general elections respectively.

15. European Parliament Elections

Voting for European Parliament elections is very soft. In 1999 over three-quarters of the electorate did not vote. In the 2004 elections over three-fifths stayed away and the Conservative and Labour parties together only achieved 48% of the vote, just 18% of the total electorate. UKIP achieved 16% of the vote, the Green Party 6% and "Other Parties" 11%. It is therefore clear that the electorate are prepared to use the European elections to send a message to the Government. This provides an excellent opportunity for the Jury Team.

The next European Parliament election is on the 4th June 2009 with nomination papers to be completed by the 7th May. The Jury Team selection process for candidates will spread over the period from mid March for six weeks.

In the June 2009 European Parliament elections there will be 12 electoral regions in the UK with nine in England and one for each of Scotland, Wales and Northern Ireland. There will be 72 seats being contested across these 12 regions with 3 seats in North East England and in Northern Ireland, 4 in Wales, 5 in the East Midlands, 6 in the South West, in Yorkshire and the Humber, in the West Midlands and in Scotland, 7 in Eastern, 8 in the North West and in London and 10 in the South East.

The elections are conducted in each region on a "party list" system (except in Northern Ireland) as decided by Tony Blair in 1999. This means that each party nominates a number of candidates up to the number of seats in the region. This system was designed to allow the Labour Party to decide which of their potential candidates should get preference in becoming an MEP as it gives central control of the order in which candidates appear on the party list. Voters can only vote for a party and not an individual candidate (for the first time in UK history).

Although designed to increase the Labour leadership's control of who would become their MEPs this system is unwittingly very helpful to the Jury Team. There is only the need to identify up to 70 candidates across all of the regions.

To convert votes into numbers of seats, England, Scotland and Wales will use the D'Hondt method of proportional representation while Northern Ireland will use Single Transferable Vote (STV). The D'Hondt procedure allocates seats in proportion to the number of votes a list receives. The Jury Team will therefore get approximately the number of seats equivalent to its share of the popular vote.

Success in these European elections will give the Jury Team great momentum towards further success in the Westminster elections.

16. Westminster Parliament Elections

As the Prime Minister still continues to have the right to use the Royal Prerogative to determine the date for the dissolution of Parliament, it is not possible to predict when the next general election will take place other than to say it will be on or before 25 days after when Parliament has to be dissolved. Parliaments can only run for five years. The current Parliament was first summoned on the 11th May 2005 and so will cease to exist at midnight on the 10th May 2010. A general election to elect the new Parliament must be held by no later than the 3rd June 2010.

Bookmakers in February 2009 are giving odds of 7/2 that the general election will occur in 2009 but show it as nine times more likely to be held in 2010 with odds of only 2/5.

The End Of The Party

In the light of the current economic circumstances it is very unlikely that there will be a general election in or before May 2009. Possible dates are to coincide with the European elections on the 4th June 2009, in October/November 2009 or in Spring 2010, especially to coincide with the local elections on the 6th May 2010.

The Jury Team is however prepared for whenever the Prime Minister will call the general election. Its technology is able to accept applications from those wanting to apply as MPs. It will decide whether to activate this for a June 2009 general election as a result of a continuing assessment of whether such a general election is probable.

In the event that the general election is not called by the Prime Minister for June 2009 then the candidate application list for MPs would be opened following what is expected to be a successful June 2009 European Parliament election for the Jury Team. There would then be a round of selection voting through the website and phone in September 2009 to decide on the Jury Team candidates for the 650 constituencies to be contested in the general election.

As it will appeal across traditional party positions the Jury Team will be able to take votes from all of the traditional parties. If it draws votes from all parties on a uniform basis, the arithmetic of elections means that to win a seat it only needs to get a proportion of votes substantially lower than the incumbent previously achieved as that incumbent will themselves lose votes.

In order to overturn a typical incumbent with a 40% share of the vote at the last general election, the Jury Team would have to take only 28.7% of the votes of that incumbent and of all the other parties to win as this would reduce the incumbent's share to only 28.5% of the total vote. There are 56 seats where the winning share of the vote was 40% or less.

The mid-point of the 646 seats in terms of the share of vote of the winner at number 323 is a share of vote of 47.3%. This would require Jury Team support by 32.1% of the electorate to win a majority of seats in the House of Commons.

The last major national party launch in the UK was that of the SDP in 1981. Their policy was to appeal to *"those from outside politics who believe that the country cannot be saved without changing the sterile and rigid framework into which the British political system has increasingly fallen in the last two decades".* Even though their communications were largely limited to the print media, as the Internet did not then exist, and by choice did not appeal across the political spectrum, they nevertheless achieved 25.3% of the vote in the 1983 general election.

Recent Independent candidates who have supported a platform against sleaze or against what they saw as improper actions by representatives of the party leaderships have done even better. In the 1997 general election Martin Bell gained <u>60.2%</u> of the vote in Tatton (in protest about the actions of the Conservative Neil Hamilton), in the 2001 general election Dr Richard Taylor gained <u>58.1%</u> of the vote in Wyre Forest (against the failed promises of a Labour minister) and in the 2005 general election Dr Peter Law gained <u>58.2%</u> in Blaenau Gwent (against Labour forcing an external candidate on the constituency).

It should also be noted that the next general election will be taking place in the context of the likelihood of a hung Parliament. The Labour Party is expected to lose some seats but could still get a majority with just 34% of the vote if the Liberal Democrats did very well. This is perhaps unlikely but as a result of the electoral discrepancies on size of constituency, turnout and share of vote between the two major parties it will also still be difficult for the Conservative Party to get a majority in the House of Commons. The best estimate is that the Conservative Party now needs to have a lead of around 9% over Labour in order to achieve a majority in the House of Commons. In these circumstances the people elected for the Jury Team will at the very least have substantial influence in the balance of power between the traditional parties.

The Jury Team believes that even in a single five year Parliamentary term it would be able to clean up the current political system and to introduce a better framework of governance for Parliament. This would then provide a robust framework of governance for whichever MPs might be elected in the Parliamentary term from 2014/5.

17. Conclusion

The Jury Team has a clear plan to use modern technology to open up and clean up politics. All of its candidates will be committed to parliament providing proper scrutiny of new legislation and to government operating ethically, efficiently, effectively and economically. They will all subscribe to the seven Nolan Principles in relation to their own conduct.

When elected as MEPs or MPs all Jury Team members will be expected to vote in favour of all proposals in line with the three Governance Principles which they will have endorsed on their application form to become a Jury Team candidate.

However on all other issues they will be able to vote in line with their best judgment as they will not be bound by any whipping system which forces them to be loyal to their party leaders rather than to their constituents and to the general population. New legislation will therefore only become law if a majority of such independent people supports it after proper scrutiny.

The Jury Team is based on the clear expression of the concerns and aspirations of the UK electorate as shown in many polls and discussions. As Gordon Brown said in his acceptance speech in May 2007 on becoming leader of the Labour Party:

"The last 10 years have taught me that the best preparation for governing is not meetings in Whitehall. The best preparation for governing is listening to the British people."

The intention of the Jury Team is not only to listen to the British people but also to involve them much more directly in the political system. This will lead to their Parliament having the capacity and structures properly to represent their interests and to their Government operating in a way in which the needs of the people are given greater priority than the needs of any political party.

"A moment comes, which comes but rarely in history, when we step out from the old to the new, when an age ends, and when the soul of a nation, long suppressed, finds utterance."
~ Jawaharlal Nehru

The End Of The Party

Jury Team Governance Proposals

1. MPs should be free to vote in line with their best judgment and should not be required to obey any party whips.

2. MPs, ministers and their political staff should be paid according to civil service pay scales, should have any expenses approved only in line with established civil service guidelines and must act according to the Nolan Principles that apply to all public bodies.

3. An independent Politicians Complaints Commission, modeled on the Independent Police Complaints Commission, with its Board appointed by a panel of designated NGOs, should be established to investigate accusations about national and local politicians, basing its judgments on the Nolan Principles that apply to all public bodies.

4. The Hayden Phillips Report recommendations on capping donations to political parties should be accepted and enforced.

5. Members of Select Committees, which hold the executive to account, should be elected by all MPs and not appointed by party whips, and should scrutinise all departmental proposals for legislation.

6. No European directive should be enacted or enforced by secondary legislation in a stricter way than is the practice in any

other European country deemed compliant for that directive by the European Commission.

7. MPs should normally serve for no more than three full terms of five years.

8. General elections should take place every five years unless a resolution of the House of Commons decides otherwise to reduce this period for particular circumstances.

9. Referendums should be called annually at all levels of government whenever requested by 5% of the relevant electorate.

10. Departments should be run by a Board chaired by the senior departmental minister but on which at least half of the directors would be appointed by a panel of designated NGOs and other stakeholders relevant to producer and consumer interests in that sector.

11. All Government statistics should be published by an independent body whose Board is appointed by a panel of designated NGOs and other stakeholders associated with the collection and use of statistics.

12. These principles should be applied at UK national level and also as far as appropriate at European Union and at devolved and local government level as well.

Chapter 2

BACKGROUND

2A. The Issues Facing the United Kingdom

1. Introduction

UK society has gone badly wrong. With the benefits of science, technology and greater human understanding our average real income after allowing for inflation is now well more than twice what it was in 1957 when Harold Macmillan said "*Let us be frank about it: most of our people have never had it so good*". However society has become increasingly fragmented, people increasingly rootless, and citizens have lost faith in Government and in the areas of life over which it presides.

This Proposal describes a way in which the governance of the UK political system can be improved. It is not designed to harp on about the many problems we see each day on the television or read about in our newspapers. It is however important to set in context the scale of the need to improve our Government system by looking at the pressures which Government is likely to have to oversee and outflank in the next few years and decades.

The Jury Team does not back specific political (rather than governance) policies because it believes that this is the responsibility of those elected. However in order to describe many of the issues facing the country, the section below shows extracts from a recent Government report, the Autumn 2008 Party

Conference speeches by the three main party leaders, reports from the key think tanks and some relevant polling data.

2. Cabinet Office Report

The Cabinet Office Strategy Unit identified a number of issues facing the UK in its February 2008 report *Realising Britain's Potential: Future Strategic Challenges for Britain.* These included:

- *globalisation*
- *economic prosperity*
- *life chances, talent and social mobility*
- *the ageing and increasing diversity of the population*
- *family life and communities*
- *crime and public safety*
- *public services*
- *climate change, and*
- *the modernisation and renewal of the constitution and democratic institutions*

The Report commented:

- *"The world around us is going to change profoundly. By 2020 China will be the 2nd and India the 6th largest economy in the world; 40% of the world's labour force will be in China and India; the world's population will have grown by another 1.2bn; and there will be increasing effects of climate change and increased pressure on global resources.*

- *There remain persistent gaps between the life chances of people from different backgrounds.*

- *There will be major demographic and social changes. As a result of ageing and net migration, the UK population is likely to grow to 67m by 2020. The number of people over 85 is expected to grow by 50% by 2020 adding further pressures to health, social care and other services.*

- *Climate change, driven by human activity, is the greatest long-term threat facing the world today.*

Taking action to mitigate it is possible, but this will require decisive international action. The UK will need to play its role both as a leader of international change but also through its own domestic commitments.

- *The increasing skew in political and civic participation - with the young and disadvantaged half as likely to participate in politics as other groups – will need to be addressed. The Government's agenda for modernising the constitution and renewing our democracy at national and local level will be central to addressing this."*

3. Party Leaders' Conference Speeches

Another perspective on the issues facing the country is shown by extracts from the speeches of the leaders of the three main political parties at their Autumn 2008 Party Conferences:

Gordon Brown - Labour Party Conference – 24th September 2008

- *I know people have real concerns about the future of the country, the future of the economy.*
- *You know, each generation believes it is living through changes their parents could never have imagined - but the collapse of banks, the credit crunch, the trebling of oil prices, the speed of technology, and the rise of Asia - nobody now can be in any doubt that we are in a different world and it's now a global age.*
- *But the continuing market turbulence shows why we now need a new settlement for these times - a settlement that we as a pro-market party must pursue.*
- *And so there are tough choices and I have to say that as a result of the events of recent weeks there are going to be tougher choices we will have to make and priorities we will have to choose.*
- *I am asking the climate change committee to report by October on the case for, by 2050 not a 60% reduction in our carbon emissions, but an 80% cut.*
- *People feel their communities are changing before their eyes and it's increasing their anxiety about crime and anti-social behaviour.*

The End Of The Party

- *For the first time ever we've got more British pensioners than British children - more people living longer on fixed incomes and worried about whether they'll need long term care.*
- *There are new pressures on parents - worrying about balancing work and family life but also about advertising aimed straight at their children and what their children are watching or downloading from the internet.*

David Cameron – Conservative Party Conference – 30th September 2008

- *In Afghanistan, the number of our troops has almost doubled but the number of helicopters has hardly increased at all. We've got troops' families living in sub-standard homes; we've got soldiers going into harm's way without the equipment they need.*
- *At the heart of the financial crisis is a simple fact. The tap marked 'borrowing' was turned on - and it was left running for too long. The debts we built up were too high. Far too high. The authorities – on both sides of the Atlantic – thought it could go on for ever.*
- *This attitude, this whole health and safety, human rights act culture, has infected every part of our life. If you're a police officer you now cannot pursue an armed criminal without first filling out a risk assessment form. Teachers can't put a plaster on a child's grazed knee without calling a first aid officer.*
- *Top-down target after top-down target, with another thirty seven targets added last year. Endless bureaucratic re-organisations, some of them contradictory, others abandoned after just a few months.*
- *When families fail, school is the way we can give children a second chance. The straightforward truth is that there aren't enough good schools, particularly secondary schools, particularly in some of our bigger towns and cities.*
- *Welfare reform is the full, pitched battle. This problem goes very deep – and dealing with it will be very tough. There are almost five million people in Britain of working age who are out of work and on benefits. That's bad for them. It's bad for our society. And it's bad for our economy.*

The End Of The Party

Nick Clegg – Liberal Democrat Conference – 17th September 2008

- *A firestorm is raging through our financial system, ignited by reckless bankers and fuelled by complacent politicians.*
- *There are huge challenges. Keeping our economy competitive as globalisation shifts the power centres of the world.*
- *Government has proved itself incapable of keeping people's data secure.*
- *Our need for dirty energy is crippling us economically. There are growing links between climate change, biofuels, and rising food prices. And inflation is fuelled by fuel. One way or another, together we are going to have to use less energy. And much less dirty energy.*
- *One in three children growing up in poverty. A million in cramped and unsafe homes where they don't get space to play. More children in prison than any other country in Western Europe. Our children are some of the most unhappy in the world.*
- *We can have a better education system, and through it a better Britain. But, inequality today isn't just about what happens at school. The crisis reaches so deep that where you are born, and who your parents are, affects everything about how your life will pan out. It even affects how long that life will be. Some day, if you're in London, get on the tube at Westminster, on the Jubilee line. Take an eastbound train towards the Docklands. Every station you pass, every time the train stops, every time the doors open and close, for every stop you travel east, life expectancy drops by a year.*
- *We are the most spied upon country in the developed world. More surveillance cameras than anywhere in the world. Parents snooped on by council officials checking up on where children spend the night. They're even putting tracking chips in our bins.*

4. <u>Think Tank Perspectives</u>

A further way of reviewing the issues facing the country is to see those identified by the major political think-tanks of various political backgrounds. The following are extracts from recent reports:

<u>Democratic Audit:</u> *It is not easy to gauge how far people in Britain feel excluded from the political process, but the latest State*

of the Nation polls, in 2004 and 2006, provide some basic answers. The 2004 poll records that 90 per cent of the public believe that 'ordinary voters' should have a great deal or a fair amount of power over government policies, but only a third feel that they have such power. Two thirds say they have a little or no power at all over their government. People also think that they and Parliament should have more power than they do.

Unlock Democracy: *In 1929, the Wall Street stock exchange collapsed, and Prime Minister Ramsay MacDonald formed a united government of all the major parties to deal with the problems we faced. 70 years on, we need unity, and this is the only way to get it. The Conservatives and Liberal Democrats keep having a go at Labour policies; and it has led to a cycle of party politics. And it is party politics that is letting down the public when we need it most. It's time for politics to be about the people, and not about the party. That's what we elected them for, and that's why we should have a national government, 'of all the talents'.*

Centre for Policy Studies: *According to the most recently published data, in September 2008, the UK's Public Sector Net Debt (including Northern Rock) is £632.7 billion. This is equivalent to 43.3% of GDP. This is a significant underestimate of the true scale of Government debt. It fails to account for the full cost of projects financed through the PFI, the extent of unfunded public sector pension liabilities, the debt incurred by Network Rail and the recent nationalisation of Bradford and Bingley. If these liabilities are included, the real level of Government debt is £1,854 billion – three times greater than the official figures. This is equivalent to 126.9% of GDP, or just under £76,000 for every household in the UK. If the cost of the recent bail-out of the UK banking sector were included, this could add up to £500 billion to the debt figure. This would imply a total debt of £2,354 billion – the equivalent of 161.1% of GDP or over £96,475 per household.* (*The Price of Irresponsibility* by Brooks Newmark MP, October 2008).

The TaxPayers' Alliance: *The performance of any organisation should be judged on the quality of its output. Judged on this basis the management of public services by politicians and civil servants has been extremely poor. Although the UK is the fifth richest country in the world:*

- *Standardised tests conducted by the OECD show that, since 2000, British 15-year-olds have fallen from 8th to 24th place in maths; from 7th to 17th in reading; and in science – an area in which the UK as a whole excels – from 4th to 14th*
- *The standard of care provided by the National Health Service is now ranked 16 in a comparison of 19 peer countries*
- *Crime levels in England and Wales are the third highest of 39 peer countries*
- *Even worse is the fact that the poor and disadvantaged get the worst education and the worst healthcare and suffer the highest rates of crime.*

Government management falls short in each of three areas:

- *Sector experience: Government departments have become so diverse that no-one could have the knowledge to manage so many different sectors. The Department for Culture, Media and Sport, for example, has 63 subsidiaries ranging from historical sites to delivery of the 2012 Olympics*
- *Management experience: none of the current cabinet has any experience of managing large businesses, and only 1 in 7 MPs has any management experience at all, let alone of giant organisations such as Government departments.*
- *Tenure: the average appointment for a Secretary of State is 2 years, for a senior civil servant 2 years and 8 months, and for a minister just 1 year and 8 months.*

(*Structure of Government No. 2*, TPA, July 2008)

Centre for Social Justice: *Our care system, despite good intentions, fails to support some of the most vulnerable people in society: children whom the state has decided cannot be brought up safely by their parents. Despite over a decade of reforming legislation and initiatives, the treatment of many children in care and those leaving the care system deserves to be a source of national shame. These children too often go on to experience lives characterised by unemployment, homelessness, mental illness and addiction:*

- *A third of homeless people were formerly in care*
- *30 per cent of children in custody have been in care*
- *23 per cent of the adult prison population has previously been in care, even though children in care and care leavers account for less than 1 per cent of the total population*

(Centre for Social Justice, 2008)

Reform: *At present the provision of schools and school places is not demand-led by parents but centrally planned by Local Education Authorities. The effect of planning decisions over the last two decades has been to reduce the number of state schools and to limit the choices available for parents. Reform has published a new ICM poll showing that three-quarters of the public think that state education in the UK is in need of fundamental review. Half of voters think that real education reform based on school choice – with taxpayer funded choice of independent as well as state schools – would be a good idea, with only a quarter thinking that it would be a bad idea. Half of Labour voters think that it would be a good idea. Young people – the group with the most recent experience of education – are the strongest supporters of school choice. 63 per cent of 18-24 year-olds think that the policy is a good idea, with only 15 per cent thinking that it would be a bad idea.*

Fabian Society: *Shifting health resources into the community - with a nurse in every school - is essential to improve health outcomes and convince the public that there is more to the NHS than hospital treatment. The new NHS should be about public health and health prevention. But if the dominance of the hospitals continues we will find ourselves unable to make substantial improvements in health outcomes, and the NHS will be ill-equipped to cope with the pressures it will face in the 21st century.*

- *Ensure that there is a school nurse in each and every primary and secondary school.*
- *Abandon the foundation trust model and integrate primary and secondary care services to form single care trusts with single budgets to remove the divide between the primary and secondary sectors.*

(*How to put public health first*, by Howard Stoate, Bryan Jones, 2008)

Institute of Economic Affairs: *While it is popularly held that markets would neglect the poor and the chronically sick, this perspective invariably ignores the comparative empirical record of the state in healthcare. Instead of recognising that the market mechanism delivers built-in incentives to level social power, erode producer capture and encourage greater inclusion, the market is causally associated with problems that are actually created by the state. In reality it is the state that neglects the poor and the chronically sick because they hold less power under its auspicies. Famously, the health economist Julian Le Grand demonstrated that in the UK, relative to need, professional and managerial groups receive more than 40% more NHS spending per illness episode than those people in semi-skilled and unskilled jobs.* (Tim Evans and Helen Evans, December 2008)

<u>Institute of Public Policy Research:</u> *Although the UK population is living longer and is in better health than ever, and older people are wealthier than they were, like the rest of the population, older people are not getting any happier. There is some evidence that older people may be becoming decreasingly satisfied, lonelier and more depressed and, due to demographic changes, there are increasing numbers of older people, many of whom are living with low levels of life satisfaction and wellbeing. This is particularly so if you are poor, isolated, in ill health, living alone, in unfit housing or rundown neighbourhoods and worse still if you are a carer or living in a care home: and all of these risk factors apply to a large proportion of the UK's older population.* (*Older People and Wellbeing* by Jessica Allen, July 2008).

<u>Politeia:</u> *In transport there are fears that things will get worse: the Government's ill - thought - out schemes for mass housing development and the influx of new people are adding to the strains on an already overburdened transport system – air, rail and road.*

Britain took a very different view to its neighbours – a distinct 'Anglo-Saxon' view - about the future of its railways in the 1960s. Virtually every other major industrial country apart from the USA chose to invest in a balanced transport system in which new motorway networks were built to meet the dramatic growth in car ownership and new high speed rail networks were created to provide more trains at competitive speeds. Britain almost uniquely in the 1960s decided that rail demand was doomed to decline and sought to limit its investment in increased transport capacity to the motorway programme. This was the 'Beeching period' in which a third of rail mileage was closed and only the West Coast mainline saw significant investment. Not surprisingly, demand for rail steadily fell from 1955 to 1982, almost as a self-fulfilling prophecy. The number of passengers using rail fell from over 1,000 million in 1955 to just 700 million in 1982. Freight tonnages suffered an even bigger collapse. (*Reviving Rail: What Strategy for Success?* By Chris Green, Politeia, February 2008)

Smith Institute: *Over 40% of all UK businesses are now homebased, according to BERR. Yet we are still planning our use of property as if we were still in the industrial age, designing-in unsustainable working practices for decades to come. A fundamental rethink amongst policy makers is necessary in order to realise the full benefits of a low carbon economy. The case for homeworking goes beyond the proven environmental benefits. There are also other tangible advantages to both employees and employers from working at home. With commutes becoming ever longer and more unpleasant, homeworking offers the opportunity for a much less stressful working experience and a better work-life balance. Individuals can work more flexibly, while cutting out the need to commute regularly gives people more free time.* (Smith Institute, 2008)

Bruges Group: *The [third and] most comprehensive layer of management over us is of course that of the European Union. It has a bureaucracy, and a kind of Parliament, but its powers could not for a moment be understood as democratically responsive. Its directives and regulations are recognised as taking precedence over Parliamentary legislation in Britain, and any appeal against them must be heard in its own European Court, in which the literal meaning of the words of an EU law is subordinated to their consonance with the basic purpose of the Union. The Commission is a fecund creator of regulations affecting many things in our everyday life, ranging from land-fill disposal of waste to the design of buses on our streets. There is, I think, no satisfactory way to quantify how much of our national life is determined by this body and estimates vary from ten percent to eighty. It is certainly true that while in principle the House of Commons should be monitoring this avalanche of legislation, much of it goes through 'on the nod', if even that.* (*Are the British a Servile People? Idealism and the EU* by Kenneth Minogue, 2008)

Open Europe: *Open Europe today condemned the EU's decision to restrict flexible employment by passing the Agency Workers Directive. Mats Persson, a spokesman for Open Europe said: "Eight of out ten of the people affected by this law will be in the UK. It is a backwards step to the 1970s, and will mean fewer jobs, just at the point when we need them most. This shows that the EU is not reforming. Instead of trying to make the EU as a whole more competitive, EU ministers seem more concerned about raising the costs of their rivals. We need flexibility and light regulation, if the EU is to survive in the 21st century. The Directive seems designed to lock member states into a corporatist way of doing business.* (Open Europe, June 2008)

Centre for European Reform: *Are the Doha trade talks finally dead? Europeans do not seem to care very much. They worry more about the impact of the global downturn on their mortgage, job and pension. Many EU Governments have also appeared distinctly unenthusiastic about trade liberalisation lately. French President Sarkozy blamed the Irish No to the Lisbon treaty on the 'overly liberal' trade policies of Trade Commissioner Peter Mandelson. During the Geneva talks, eight other EU countries lined up behind France (including Italy, Greece, Poland and Hungary). They argued that Mandelson's first responsibility was to protect European jobs and incomes – in particular in the farm sector – not to finish a round of trade talks of dubious economic value. Would the failure of Doha be a disaster for Europe? Not on the face of it. With many of its biggest trading partners – China, Russia, ASEAN, the EFTA countries – the EU has special agreements on trade and investment, or is in the process of negotiating them (albeit with limited success). And many poorer countries may be more willing to grant the EU better access to their markets on a bilateral basis – without having to extend the same* privileges to China. (Should Europeans care about Doha? by Katinka Barysch, July 2008)

Policy Network: *For once there is a vision of Europe's future that Britain shares. It is not directly about the future of the European Union, though I believe it is highly relevant to it. Rather it is a striking mood of pessimism about the social trends in our societies: we may be the first generation since the great advance of material progress which began with the industrial revolution that believes life will not be as good for our children and grandchildren as it has been for us. At the heart of this pessimism there is a profound paradox. Surveys repeatedly show high levels of self-reported individual life satisfaction and happiness. These have been broadly stable in the most prosperous European countries for a generation, with no tendency to rise once a certain level of material prosperity is attained: a fact that is significant for the growing debate about "wellbeing" in affluent societies. But high life satisfaction and happiness goes alongside quite deep pessimism about prospects for the long term.* (*Social pessimism - The new social reality of Europe* by Roger Liddle, October 2008)

Demos: *Both public servants and politicians will face challenges in developing a more agile set of public institutions. Policy makers at the heart of Government will need to become much more comfortable with the idea of innovation being driven by frontline workers – central agencies need to become talent spotters for new ideas and initiatives or risk becoming bottlenecks. Joining up Government around outcomes will require a significant investment of political and managerial leadership to break down entrenched barriers. Effective shaping of the future environment will often require public sector leaders to take an unfashionably long view of policy problems.* (*Towards Agile Government* by Simon Parker and Jamie Bartlett, 2008)

5. The Electorate's Perspective

There are no simple answers to the questions facing modern societies, especially not from a "bloc" view of many issues compacted together to try to fit in with traditional party philosophies. Socialism is discredited in New Labour. Capitalism is unloved by the Conservative Party leadership. Social democracy leads to stagnation and a dangerous dependence of the bottom quarter of society on those above them and on the state. Individualism corrodes the bonds of community and, even for successful individuals, feels selfish and unsatisfying.

There are many areas which have been identified as generating serious concern among voters. The Ipsos/MORI poll for August 2008 showed the following percentages of voters who responded positively, unprompted, to the two questions: *"What would you say is the most important issue facing Britain today?"* and *"What do you see as other important issues facing Britain today?"*

It is noticeable that many of the responses are different or in a different order (e.g. climate change/environment) from those identified by the Cabinet Office and some of the think tanks:

	%
Crime/Law & Order/Violence/Vandalism	47
Economy/Economic Situation	41
Inflation/Prices	26
Race Relations/Immigration/Immigrants	25
NHS/Hospitals/Health Care	15
Defence/Foreign Affairs/International Terrorism	15
Housing	13
Education	12
Petrol Prices/Fuel	10
Morality/Individual Behaviour	9
Unemployment/Factory Closure/Lack of Industry	7
Pollution/Environment	7
Drug Abuse	7
Poverty/Inequality	6
Taxation	5
Low Pay/Minimum Wage/Fair Wages	4

People do not generally see the UK Government as the dominant influence in their lives. In a November 2006 survey, Ipsos/MORI asked: *"From this list, which two or three of the following do you believe have most impact on people's everyday lives?"* (Wales/Scotland/Northern Ireland questions* were only asked in the respective areas):

	%
Media	54
Local Councils	48
Business	37
Westminster Parliament	26
Prime Minister	24
Civil Service	20
European Union	20
Cabinet	7
National Assembly for Wales*	2
Scottish Parliament*	1
Northern Ireland Assembly*	1

This is also illustrated in another Ipsos/MORI poll from September 2007 which showed that, other than having a higher salary, better quality uses of leisure time are the most important factors people believe would increase their happiness. The responses to the question: "*Which four or five of the following things do you think would make you happier?*" were:

	%
More time with family	37
Earning double what I do now	35
Better health	30
More time with friends	23
More traveling	22
More time for leisure/sport	21
Better community spirit	19
Having a happy marriage	17
More contact with nature	16
Better housing	15
Learning new skills	13
Moving abroad	12
Moving jobs	6
More time to think/be alone	5

6. Political Leaders' Unfulfilled Aspirations

These matters have, perhaps surprisingly, been recognised by the leaders of all of the three main political parties although their words have not been matched by the actions of themselves or their parties:

In his May 2007 speech on becoming leader of the Labour Party, Gordon Brown stated that:

> *We must address new challenges today – challenges very different and more pressing to which we must respond:*
>
> > *To those who feel the political system doesn't listen and doesn't care;*
> >
> > *To those who feel powerless and have lost faith;*
> >
> > *To those who feel Westminster is a distant place and politics simply a spectator sport:*

And to build trust in our democracy, we need a more open form of dialogue for citizens and politicians to genuinely debate problems and solutions.

Similarly in his speech to the Conservative Party Conference in October 2008, David Cameron said:

But no-one will ever take lectures from politicians about responsibility unless we put our own house in order. That means sorting out our broken politics. People are sick of it. Sick of the sleaze, sick of the cynicism. Copper-bottomed pensions. Plasma screen TVs on the taxpayer. Expenses and allowances that wouldn't stand for one second in the private sector.

This isn't a Conservative problem, a Labour problem or a Liberal Democrat problem. It is a Westminster problem, and we've all got to sort it out. In the end, this is about the judgment to see how important this issue is for the credibility of politics and politicians. And it's about having the character to take on vested interests inside your own party.

On the same theme, at the Liberal Democrat Conference in September 2008, Nick Clegg said:

And there are problems in Britain today. Too many. Families stuck in grinding poverty. Liberty taken and abused by Government officials. Climate change starting to tighten its deathly grip. But they aren't problems with the British people. They're problems faced by the British people. We are not the problem. It's the system that's the problem.

No wonder people are tired of politics. Tired of a system that swings like a pendulum between two establishment parties. Tired of the same old politicians, the same old fake choices, the same old feeling that nothing ever changes. But this isn't a story of indifference. People do care about issues. Climate change. Poverty. Their local school or hospital. There are marches and campaigns and petitions launched every day of the week. People care. They just don't care about politicians. So this is the end of the line for politics-as-usual. If we want a political system that works for the future, we need to start again. From scratch.

The establishment parties will manipulate the system to get the power they want. But they'll never change it. They like having power and privilege sewn up between a few chums in the Westminster bubble.

7. The Failure to Reform the Current Party Political System

There is therefore agreement that the current party political system is at the root of the UK's problems because it fails to reflect the will of the people, to allow informed discussion of new laws and to have sensible and proportionate management of the areas of the country's life with which the Government is involved.

However the current system has clearly proven itself incapable of reform from within.

Indeed the existing political parties have deliberately tried to make it even harder for Independents to stand. The Electoral Commission stated in a 2003 report which discussed the effects of the Political Parties, Elections and Referendums Act 2000 (PPERA):

> *"Independents*
>
> *4.11 Independents have a long-standing place in the political system in the UK and have traditionally been an important force in local elections. However, the regime introduced by PPERA has introduced significant change. Between 1969 and 2001, all candidates standing at election in the UK were entitled to use a description, and the change introduced by PPERA is a fundamental shift that many independent candidates feel discriminates against them. Under the existing system, the only way that independent candidates can use a description is by registering the description as a party name (perhaps by registering a friend or supporter as a second party officer).*
>
> *4.12 Perhaps unsurprisingly, in a House of Commons dominated by party members, little or no consideration appeared to have been given during the passage of PPERA*

> *to the impact the legislation would have on independents. During the 2001 election campaign, some independent candidates raised concerns with the Commission that the new legislation had created a significant disadvantage in severely constraining the wording they could use on ballot papers. Many of those who made their views known in advance of this review expressed the opinion that PPERA had gone 'too far' and had failed to strike the right balance between avoiding confusion for voters and enabling candidates to describe themselves effectively on the ballot paper."*

The existing political parties have tried to ignore the clearly expressed views of the electorate for more dynamic and less "lobby fodder" politics. The parties have tried to stop the emergence of Independent candidates.

However people in the UK do not like to see independence penalised as an underdog. By organising Independent candidates at a national level the Jury Team will reinvigorate UK politics by providing voters with the opportunity to elect independent people from outside the existing parties who are close to their community and who are pledged to improve the governance of the country.

2B. History of Parliament and Government

1. The Early Years

From the signing of the Magna Carta almost 800 years ago the British people have fought and generally won the battle to tame the autocratic power of those set over them. Building upon Anglo Saxon traditions, King John at Runnymede accepted that he was subject to the law as well as benefiting from the "divine right of kings". Many centuries of conflict followed between the monarch and those representing the people. The British also repelled those from other countries who wished to impose autocracy upon them.

Gradually the kings and queens began to appreciate that they required popular support. They could no longer rely on apparently being anointed and realised that they needed to bring together an assembly to give themselves legitimacy. Their powers and this Parliament evolved into our modern system of Government.

2. The Evolution of Parliament

The word Parliament originally meant a "talk" with the word being used in the 13th century to describe after-dinner discussions between monks in their cloisters. In 1239 the Benedictine monk Matthew Paris applied the term to a council meeting between prelates, earls, and barons. Modern Parliaments trace their history to the 13th century when the sheriffs of English counties sent knights to the king to provide advice on financial matters. These assemblies were based on the proceedings of the City of London's Common Council. The Parliament called in 1295 is widely regarded as the first representative Parliament and included two knights from each county, two burgesses from each borough, and two citizens from each city.

Early in the 14th century the practice developed of conducting debates between the lords spiritual and temporal in one chamber, or "house", and between the knights and burgesses in another. Meanwhile, the greater cohesion of the monarch's Privy (private) Council achieved in the 14th century separated it in practice from Parliament. Bills, if assented to by the monarch, became Acts of Parliament. For five hundred years following Magna Carta, Parliament continued to operate on the basis of individuals being elected to represent their constituencies and to use their best judgment in deciding on issues.

3. Development of Political Parties

Political parties began developing at the beginning of the 1700's, initially the Whigs (horse thieves) and then to counter them the Tories (papist outlaws). These parties were designed not to achieve particular policies for the good of the nation but to provide greater Parliamentary pressure against the king.

The parties were however very fluid until after the 1832 Reform Act which extended the franchise and increased the need for campaigning. This led to local registration societies and then constituency associations, and political parties developed for electoral purposes. In Parliament, as the scope of Government grew from the mid-Victorian time onwards, the party in power increasingly "whipped" its MPs to support it (the word "whip" coming from the use of the same word in hunting as the person who gathers or "whips in" the hounds). After the 1872 Ballot Act, which introduced secret ballots for general elections, the powers of the parties slowly increased. In HMS Pinafore (1878) W. S. Gilbert wrote:

"I always voted at my party's call.
And I never thought of thinking for myself at all."

Throughout the Victorian era private members' bills nevertheless remained a vital source of legislation and party allegiance remained much weaker than now. Subsequently during the 20th Century "whipping" in Parliament inexorably strengthened and for election campaigns a centrally directed party system developed in order to run national campaigns and identify likely local supporters.

4. Development of the Cabinet

In medieval times the monarch appointed, and operated through, a Privy Council. The main Government function was the collection and disbursement of taxes, with the Exchequer (Treasury) being given a dominant role. Historically the Cabinet began as a sub-group of the Privy Council with the name meaning a small and private room used as a study or retreat. The *OED* credits Francis Bacon in his *Essays* (1605) with the first use of "Cabinet Council", where it is described as a foreign habit, of which he disapproves: *"For which inconveniences, the doctrine of Italy, and practice of France, in some kings' times, hath introduced Cabinet counsels; a remedy worse than the disease"*. Almost certainly Bacon's problem with Cabinets was that they deliberated in private rather than in the open court where all could hear the issues.

Charles I began a formal "Cabinet Council" from his accession in 1625 as his Privy Council was evidently not private enough. The first recorded use of "Cabinet" by itself for such a body comes from 1644 and is again hostile and associates the term with dubious foreign practices. The Cabinet gradually emerged as the main coordinator of the executive functions of Government.

The Act of Settlement with Scotland in 1701 specified that no "*placemen of the monarch*", i.e. ministers, could sit as MPs but this was repealed in 1705. We would otherwise have a system very much like the modern US one.

During the 17th and 18th Centuries new departments of state were slowly introduced but remained very small with typically no more than 30 staff right through to mid-Victorian times. For those simple circumstances, in 1854, Northcote and Trevelyan introduced their reforms of the civil service. These were based on the Chinese Mandarin system, with the senior grades being filled by young men recruited from the best universities for a lifetime career. Ministers oversaw them and reported to Parliament.

Government grew substantially in the late 1800's and early 1900's with the introduction of areas such as social insurance but both departmental structures and Cabinet meetings were described right up until the First World War as having a country house party atmosphere. The civil service increased from 21,000 in 1832 to 282,000 in 1914.

In 1916 a formal Cabinet system was introduced with agendas and minutes. During the First and Second World Wars many new people were brought temporarily into Government to deal with the urgent enemy threat but otherwise the Government machine continued to consolidate along the lines of the Northcote-Trevelyan reforms.

5. The US Mirrors the 18th Century UK Position

The US Constitution, drafted in 1783, was very much based on the then UK unwritten constitution and is an interesting description of the structures then in place in the UK. The President (the equivalent of the monarch) was given essentially the same powers as the monarch, as this was the system that the Revolutionaries knew, but they decided that their problems of unfair representation or taxation could be solved if the President were elected. As a result the elected President assumed the same powers as the monarch, acting as commander-in-chief, being in charge of the executive branch and appointing the judiciary.

This is discussed in a letter from Thomas Jefferson to James Sullivan in 1797:

Where a constitution, like ours, wears a mixed aspect of monarchy and republicanism, its citizens will naturally divide into two classes of sentiment, according as their tone of body or mind, their habits, connections and callings, induce them to wish to strengthen either the monarchical or the republican features of the constitution. Some will consider it as an elective monarchy, which had better be made hereditary, and therefore endeavor to lead towards that all the forms and principles of its administration. Others will view it as an energetic republic, turning in all its points on the pivot of free and frequent elections."

The one area that is often cited as being different in structure between the US and the UK is that the UK has a Parliamentary Government whereas in the US the members of the Cabinet, and consequently all administrative officers such as ambassadors and commissioners, are appointed by the President. However this is in fact also just a reflection of the process in 18th Century England when the King appointed the Privy Council, the main executive arm of the Government from which the Cabinet was drawn, which did not then necessarily have to reflect the views of Parliament and certainly not of the House of Commons.

The US Constitution set this position in stone so that the (now elected) President/Monarch could appoint his own Cabinet without worrying about the composition of Congress (Parliament). The US Cabinet still does not function as a legislative body but rather keeps its primary role as the group of ministers who run the major departments (only seven) and form an unofficial advisory council to the President, as it was in the 18th Century to the King.

These modern constitutional differences between the two countries highlight how the separation of legislative and executive powers, which ironically was a royalist concept, was enshrined in the US Constitution but has been substantially eroded in the UK.

6. The Coalescing of Parliament and Government

The executive and the legislature in the UK are now essentially amalgamated. In the early 19th Century UK monarchs continued to appoint their Privy Council, which had the main executive authority, but they began to adjust the composition of the Privy Council according to that of Parliament whose popular legitimacy increased with the extension of the electoral franchise. The convention that Governments would automatically resign if they lost an election developed, taking away some power of appointment from the monarch.

In the UK, without a written constitution, the executive and legislature continued to coalesce, compared with the defined US position, with Queen Victoria eventually being required constitutionally to appoint her Cabinet from those supported by the House of Commons.

"The reason for alarm is not that the English executive is too strong, for weak Government generally means bad administration, but that our English executive is, as a general rule, becoming more and more the representative of a party rather than the guide of a country"
~ Albert Venn Dicey, 1885

7. Appointment of the Prime Minister and Cabinet

The final loss of monarchical appointment power is fairly recent. Winston Churchill was appointed as Prime Minister in 1940 without any public discussion. Even the choice of Alec Douglas-Home as Prime Minister in 1963 was one which had not been tested in Parliament or by a party election.

The election of MPs to the House of Commons is now little more than an election on party lines of people not known to the electorate whose main role is to signal who should become the head of the Government. This is similar to the US Electoral College in choosing the President. Nowadays each major political party has an agreed method for electing its leader and the party with a majority in the House of Commons has its leader appointed as Prime Minister.

In theory the Prime Minister is first among equals (primus/a inter pares). However, the Prime Minister is the person who essentially exercises the monarch's prerogative and executive powers which include areas such as the dissolution of Parliament, declaration of war, command of the armed forces and espionage agencies and appointments to senior positions in many areas of Government. This means that in practice the Prime Minister is clearly the leader of the Cabinet.

The Prime Minister essentially recommends the appointment of the Cabinet to the monarch. Until well into the 20th Century, when an MP was appointed as a minister he had to resign as an MP and seek re-election. This provided a substantial check on ministerial appointments. However any restrictions on the power of Prime Ministers to appoint MPs or Lords as ministers have now disappeared and the Prime Minister has almost unfettered discretion to run the Government as he or she sees fit and to hire and fire all of the senior players.

Baroness Helena Kennedy, Chair of the 2006 Power Inquiry, has said:

"Experience has taught us a lot of important lessons about power. Particularly political power. The great Lord Acton's words are often quoted: 'Power corrupts and absolute power corrupts absolutely'. And I have now developed it into 'Power is delightful and absolute power is absolutely delightful'."

In her introduction to the Power Inquiry report she also stated:

"The politicos have no idea of the extent of the alienation that is out there"

8. <u>The Domination of Power</u>

This system gives the party with a Parliamentary majority access to all of the levers of state. All ministers, not just the Prime Minister, act in the name of the monarch, and therefore command absolutely the organs of the state such as the armed forces. They have greater powers of decision and patronage than in almost any other Western democracy. Their intentions are normally rubber stamped by their party's MPs through the whipping system.

"The British constitution is an elective dictatorship"
Lord Hailsham, 1978

As the Government machine has become stronger, Parliament has become weaker. Being the leader of the majority party in Parliament, the Prime Minister can normally expect all of his or her Government's legislative proposals to be supported by calling on the Whips to seek votes from the party's Members of Parliament, by definition the majority of the House of Commons, to support his or her views. Patronage gives the Prime Minister considerable coercive power both with members of the Government who depend on him or her for promotion and also with backbench MPs, especially those who hope to achieve ministerial office or a role as a member or chairman of a Select Committee.

In cases where MPs try to stand up to their party such as during the debates on the Maastricht Treaty or on the introduction of 42-day detention, massive pressure is brought to bear on all MPs, even from different parties, to support the Government.

In an article about the House of Commons vote on 42-day detention Jim Pickard and Jimmy Burns wrote in The Financial Times in June 2008:

"Diane Abbott, a leading Labour rebel in last night's vote, was a picture of anger and despair as she described the desperate efforts by government whips to win support for the 42-day detention plan through a series of concessions, bribes and threats. 'Is it right that our civil liberties should be traded in this kind of bazaar?' she asked. The rumours included one unnamed MP being offered softer European Union sanctions against Cuba and another losing her 'special envoy' status.

Ministers, whips and the prime minister have spent recent days pleading with backbenchers in person and by phone to step into line. They offered not only carrots but also - in the words of one backbencher – 'bone crunching pressure'."

Rather than ministers having the objective of trying to achieve the solution which best represents the popular and indeed expert will of properly elected Members of Parliament, their overriding objective becomes the preservation of the Government's reputation.

Similarly when facing difficult issues a Prime Minister may bring forward legislation which he knows will be popular with his backbench MPs in order to divert them and ensure their solidarity. A recent example of this was the Fox Hunting Bill which took many hours of Parliamentary time in the main chamber and in committees at a time when Tony Blair otherwise faced severe criticism from Labour MPs about the Iraq War and various domestic policies.

As Prime Minister Disraeli said:

"A Government is an organised hypocrisy."

9. The Modern Cabinet System

The Cabinet has an input into the legislative programme and is meant to be the country's main executive decision making body. Members of the Cabinet are collectively responsible for decisions taken in Cabinet and all members of the Government, whether in the Cabinet or junior ministers, must publicly support the policy of the Government, regardless of any private reservations.

Although, in theory, all Cabinet decisions are taken collectively by the Cabinet, in practice most decisions are delegated to the various sub-committees of the Cabinet which rarely report to the full Cabinet on their findings and recommendations. Matters are normally only referred to the full Cabinet if a disagreement remains to be resolved or the issue is so important that the Cabinet should decide it anyway. Cabinet deliberations are secret and documents dealt with in Cabinet are confidential. Most of the documentation associated with Cabinet meetings will only be publicly released a considerable period later, normally after thirty years.

The functions of Cabinet have also changed. Cabinet meetings now rarely discuss any major issues or make decisions contrary to those already taken elsewhere. In his chapter of the compilation *The British Constitution in the Twentieth Century* edited by Vernon Bogdanor, Anthony Seldon describes how the main feature of the Cabinet since the 1980s has been presentation and media management:

"a purely presentational function, with meetings always ending just in time to feed the lunch-time news bulletins"

The constitutional expert Sir Bernard Crick said in 2003:

"We need a return to the old conventions of cabinet Government with the prime minister as 'first among equals', not 'democratic dictator' or pseudo-president."

10. The Kitchen Cabinet

The historic process of moving from a Privy Council to a Cabinet has repeated itself in recent times. Prime Ministers (now acting as monarchs in function) have felt the need to have their own inner group, a Kitchen Cabinet. Since the 1970's, Wilson, Callaghan, Thatcher, Major, Blair and Brown all had confidants and influential advisers who were not in the official Cabinet. The influence of these advisers is well documented, not least in the memoirs they tend to write on leaving office in order to capitalise on their brief period in the corridors of power.

Britain consequently has a very centralised political system which has substantial control over many aspects of life with local areas and councils having minimal autonomy. This is in contrast to the position even in other parliamentary systems such as Australia, Canada or India where states and provinces have specific power over many aspects of Government. Similarly in France the *départements* and local *mairies* are powerful and in Germany there is a strong federal structure with the German constitution specifically separating the executive and legislative branches as in the United States.

11. Civil Society

One great strength of the UK however is the breadth of civil society outside of the Government, operating through what are generally described as non-governmental organisations ("NGOs"). These include registered charities, community groups, women's organisations, faith-based organisations, professional associations, trade unions, self-help groups, social movements, business associations, coalitions and advocacy groups. Such organisations have a tremendous sense of independence and integrity.

For instance in 2008 there were about 170,000 main charities with a total income of £46 billion, over a quarter more than the country's defence budget, with 600,000 paid staff. They have 900,000 trustees and millions of other volunteers, all giving their time for nothing. Some enjoy huge individual support with the National Trust having over 3.5 million members and the Royal Society for the Protection of Birds having over one million, double the membership of all political parties combined.

There are also many organisations with the "Royal" accolade which range from charities such as the Royal Society for the Prevention of Cruelty to Animals to a wide series of expert societies such as the Royal Astronomical Society, Royal Geographical Society, Royal Horticultural Society, Royal Philatelic Society and Royal Photographic Society. Similarly there are many "Chartered" bodies, normally Institutes, which are for members of a particular profession ranging through the alphabet from Accountancy and Arbitration to Taxation and Waste Management.

There are additionally a vast range of other groups operating locally which provide a bedrock of UK society. These include the Scout Association and Girlguiding UK, which together have more than a million members, Boys Brigade, Salvation Army, Rotary International, Lions Clubs, Samaritans, St John Ambulance, Wildlife Trusts and car, railway, music, drama and other hobby interest societies.

The contrast between the ethos and practice of these many voluntary organisations and the world of politics is stark. There is no doubt that the standards and experience of civil society can be better used in providing potential Parliamentary candidates and in helping to choose those who run our major departments of state.

2C. The Current Party Political System and Elections

"The Emperor has no clothes!"
~ The Child, Hans Christian Andersen

1. The Party System

The Encyclopedia Britannica states:

"Political parties, like all organisations, tend to manipulate their members, to bring them under the control of an inner circle of leaders that often perpetuates itself. Members tend to be manipulated by powerful committees containing cliques of influential party leaders. In mass-based parties, leaders are chosen by the members, but incumbents are very often re-elected because they control the party apparatus, using it to ensure their continuation in power.

The End Of The Party

Democratic political systems, while performing the function of representation, thus rest more or less on the competition of rival oligarchies."

The concept of loyalty to a political party can be seen as completely opposite to what it should mean to be a democratic politician whose prime responsibility is to represent his or her constituents. Their party forces politicians first to be loyal to it and only then to the public.

MPs may try to be loyal to their constituents but there is a line they cannot cross if it becomes a party matter. A graphic example of this has been the recent proposed closure of local post offices where Labour MPs sympathised with their constituents and said in writing that they would support them but actually voted for the closure programme in the Commons.

2. The Key Objective of Modern Political Parties

"Senior politicians and their political parties are power-crazed for electoral victory and powerless when it comes to understanding the content and ideas required of political leadership."
~ President Richard Weizsacker of Germany

Nowadays it appears that more time, money and effort is put into getting elected than actually working for the people supposedly represented. People see that political parties have as their "bottom line" the winning of elections.

This perception was confirmed by Tony Blair in his speech to the TUC in September 1995: *"But what has come home to me more than anything else is the utter futility of Opposition. I did not join the Labour Party to protest. I joined it as a party of Government and I will make sure that it is a party of Government."*

Given statements like these it is not surprising that a 2001 election survey showed that 60% of the UK electorate felt that the parties were *"more interested in winning elections than in governing afterwards"*.

People perceive that what may be best for the party leaders in pursuit of their own or their party's self-interest may well conflict with the public good and that if it does then it is unlikely that the public good will win.

3. The Growth of the Central Party Organisations

Parliament operated successfully during much of the Victorian era with independent MPs themselves deciding how to vote. The Victorian electoral reforms extending the franchise however supplied many more electors which led to the formation of local party constituency associations which were set up to record the names of the electorate and their voting intentions.

Local election expenses were circumscribed by the 1883 Corrupt Practices Act. However as central party organisations hardly existed in the late Victorian era then no restrictions were put on central electoral expenditure.

The central party political organisations have consequently become powerful and even now have minimal limits on their expenditure other than during the short election campaign period itself.

4. The Parties in the Country

The local membership of political parties has hugely decreased from over 3 million in the 1960s to now less than 1% of the UK population. There are many parts of the country where either the Labour or Conservative parties (and sometimes both) no longer have viable constituency associations.

The remaining local organisations are no longer typical of the electorate in terms of age, gender and ethnic background in any of the major parties. The average age of Conservative Party members is said to be 62 and of Labour Party members to be 50.

Local parties are now just shells of political enthusiasts, often motivated to belong mainly by the social networking opportunities, who have little influence on policy development. Their only real task is to select their Member of Parliament but this typically takes place only every 10-15 years when they anyway have to choose between a centrally sanctioned group of people.

The grass-roots party political system therefore now has little legitimacy. In July 1999 The Economist stated:

"Belonging to a British political party is more like being a supporter of some charity: you may pay a membership fee, but will not necessarily attend meetings or help to turn out the vote at election time".

John Major wrote in 2003:

"At the grass roots, our political parties are shrinking in membership from mass movements to the size of special interest groups. The broad mass of the nation is detached from politics. Many feel a distaste for it. All the party machines are moribund, near-bankrupt, unrepresentative and ill-equipped to enthuse the electorate."

Jackie Ashley, daughter of a Labour MP, said in 2003:

"You cannot have a Parliamentary system based on political parties if across most of the country they have ceased to exist."

5. <u>The Lack of Proper Representation</u>

At local level, individual party candidates play only a minimal role in the overall result and even the national election campaigns address only a small proportion of the issues facing the country.

Democracy is essentially a way to select leaders. It has stood the test of time against more autocratic systems. However one of its necessary tests is that it should be able to demonstrate greater strength than the alternative of using a lottery, as practiced by the Greeks, to select who should make decisions on behalf of the rest of the country. A lottery at least ensures that all sections of the community have an equal chance of being selected which is sadly not true for our current democracy.

Parliament should represent the population as well as possible in terms of gender, ethnicity and occupational experience. However in Parliament women currently have only about 40% of their proper representation. Similarly ethnic minorities have only about 30% of what would be required to reflect the ethnicity of the population as a whole. The inability of the party political system to provide sufficient women or ethnic minority candidates means that those groups have a strong argument in denying the legitimacy of Parliament. The use of single member constituencies means that constituencies have little flexibility in their choice of candidates and therefore tend to choose a white male if they are only given one shot at who should be selected to fight for their party.

This point was made clearly in November 2008 by Trevor Philips, Chairman of the Equality and Human Rights Commission, who told BBC Radio 4's Today programme: *"The political system has a problem....My point is a very simple one - the political system is to some extent closed to outsiders, to people who are not of a particular stamp. This is not just about race, this is a wider point that our leadership class is really basically white, male and professional. It is very hard for women to break in and very hard for working-class people to get to the higher reaches of parties."*

6. The Representation of Women

From 1922, when the first two women MPs were elected, until 1959, women accounted for no more than 4% of all MPs. This figure gradually rose to 9% in the 1992 election and then approximately doubled to 18% in 1997 and 2001.

In the 2005 election there were 433 women candidates from the three main parties: 166 Labour, 122 Conservative and 145 Liberal Democrat. The number of women MPs increased by 10 over the number in 2001 to 128, comprising 98 Labour (28% of their party), 17 Conservative (9%), 10 Liberal Democrat (16%) and 3 representing Northern Ireland parties. The 38 new women MPs made up nearly a third of the new intake and the new total of 128 women MPs represents 20% of the House of Commons. Although Labour did its best with the election of 26 new women MPs this was only three more than the number of women Labour MPs who retired or were beaten in the election.

In his 2005 leadership election, David Cameron ruled out all women shortlists, as Iain Duncan Smith had done before, knowing that this was usually unpopular with the local membership who would soon vote on whether they wanted him as their leader. Charles Kennedy was in contrast very clear about wanting to have quantity guarantees for women but he, followed by Menzies

Campbell when he became leader, was unable to get his party to accept the necessary regulations.

At the next general election, the Liberal Democrats and Conservatives look set to improve their own parties' gender balance. However the potential loss of dozens of marginal seats currently held by female Labour MPs would offset any gains in the overall representation of women in the House. If, as currently expected, Labour does not do well in the next general election then a large number of its current women MPs, who largely hold less safe seats, are likely to be eliminated from Parliament. This means that given the resistance of other parties in selecting female candidates then it is likely that the proportion of women in Parliament from the traditional parties will be reduced after the next general election unless there is a substantial change in the political system. This is a further reason why it is important for the Jury Team to succeed.

The Electoral Reform Society confirmed in its research published in July 2008 that, with the current party political system, there is no prospect of increasing the number of women MPs at the next election. Beatrice Barleon, the Electoral Reform Society's Women's Officer, said: *"The parties talk a lot about the need for greater equality but in every likely scenario for the next election, they can't deliver"*.

7. <u>The Representation of Ethnic Minorities</u>

Parties are also not usually good at embracing people from ethnic minorities. As well as being a new element coming into a traditional hierarchy, if the ethnic group has a particular policy view then this may not easily fit with the rest of the party. This is especially so on issues such as immigration control, war or the rights of asylum seekers where an ethnic group may well have a different view from the party leadership, even if it subscribes to many of the party's other policies.

There were 117 ethnic minority candidates at the 2005 election, 34 from Labour, 41 from the Conservative Party and 42 from the Liberal Democrats. However the new total of 15 non-white MPs (13 Labour and two Conservative) was only three more than the 12 (all Labour) chosen in 2001. They represented just 2.3% of the 646 MPs against the national ethnic minority representation of 7+%.

In January 2009 Trevor Philips, Chairman of the Equality and Human Rights Commission, said that *"Parliament may be the pumping heart of our democracy, but its lifeblood is white, straight and male. That has to change."*

8. <u>The Representation of Minority Parties</u>

In all of the regional assemblies, mayoral elections and European Parliamentary contests which have been established since 1997, proportional representation is used in order to give a fairer result and to allow minor parties, such as the Greens, to be represented.

Both major parties at Westminster have resisted this for general elections without explicitly explaining why. However it is clear that their real reason for this failure is that they realise that introducing proportional representation at Westminster would lead to both major parties losing a substantial number of their current MPs who, perhaps understandably from their point of view, act like turkeys who do not want to vote for Christmas.

9. <u>The Narrow Focus of Election Campaigning</u>

"Élections - piège à cons" (Elections - a trap for idiots)
~ French 1968 May revolt:

UK general election campaigns are formally quite short but there is essentially continuous campaigning for several years before each election. People are nowadays much less hidebound by the political voting choices of their class or parents with most of the electorate not having any strong party political convictions.

The first past the post (FPTP) system operating in individual constituencies means that most votes are wasted as they are cast in the over three quarters of Parliamentary seats which are safe under any likely political balance between the two main parties.

The FPTP system concentrates electoral power in the target constituencies which represent only about 20% of the total of 646 seats. Within these seats only about 10% of the voters are seen as key as they may be persuaded to change their voting allegiance. This means that just 10% of 20%, being 2%, of the 45 million registered voters are actually targeted. These 900,000 people are bombarded by personalised messages, most of which do not relate to policy but to the personal characteristics of the leadership which also dominate the broadcast and press media.

As a US campaign leader once said:

"You can fool some of the people all of the time, and those are the ones you should concentrate on"

For the 2005 general election the Conservatives set up a call centre in the Midlands and had a staff of 50 in London for the same purpose. They used the "Voter Vault" system pioneered by Karl Rove, George W. Bush's Campaign Manager. Together with Experian, the people data services company, this identified the most likely floating voters in each marginal seat. These 838,000 people received a substantially enhanced level of direct mail, telephone calls, CDs/DVDs and visits from local campaigners. The Conservatives used ORB for their main polling which took place in the 130 Labour held and 33 Liberal Democrat held target seats. During the main campaign they researched 500 voters every night to give a rolling 1,500 voter sample by combining three days of polling. They also conducted about 90 focus groups in target seats.

The Labour Party communications centre in Gosforth employed over 120 people. During the campaign it made more than 2 million phone calls and sent out 10 million items of direct mail. For identifying floating voters Labour used a similar system to the Conservatives called Contact. The party's objective was to have seven contacts with each target voter by polling day. Labour concentrated on Feedback from 130 marginal constituencies and produced a monthly poll and then six tracking polls during the four weeks of the actual campaign. They had frequent focus groups with one among target voters every night and with Philip Gould also arranging up to four focus groups a week.

It becomes increasingly difficult for most people to know what a party stands for as the message is honed relentlessly for the floating voters. In contrast to the overriding efforts expended by the parties on the 2% of floating voters, only a fifth of all voters received a visit in 2005 from a party member according to the British Election Study.

10. Party Funding

The funding of political parties has become a major issue. The key reason for this is because of the centralised power of the political parties. It is the justified belief that one or at most a few people can make political decisions with no real challenge from Parliament that makes it possible for there to be such suspicion about donations.

If candidates were elected as independent individuals then party political funding would no longer be as important. Coupled with the need for any significant policy changes to be debated properly in Parliament or subject to independent scrutiny within departments, there would be less suspicion that policies were being corrupted by donations.

11. The Use of Issues in Campaigning

Anthony Downs, the political scientist, said in 1957:

"Competition between the two main parties just entails both situating themselves towards the middle of the political spectrum to maximise their market share".

While the vast majority of the electorate remains interested in national and local issues, most people in the UK feel that they do not have a say in how the country is run. Three fifths of the public can no longer see any real difference between the main political parties. Political debate is seen as hollowed out.

For instance, following the House of Commons vote on the 10 pence income tax rate in April 2008, Camilla Cavendish wrote in The Times:

"Mr Brown has rescued his Finance Bill. But this arcane-sounding row has lost him something more profound. He has been exposed as putting political advantage before principle even on the issue that he is supposed to care most about - poverty. He only introduced the 10p band in the first place to wrong-foot the

Opposition. He abolished it for the same reason. It has been, from start to finish, a brazen political fiddle."

When there are two main parties they will tend to adjust their policies, candidates and leaders to maximise their popular vote. This means that they will always tend to the middle and find it difficult to espouse any strong policies. This can be seen by considering the political spectrum from left to right. Such a line was used in economics by Harold Hotelling to explain how two shops might locate in a single street in order to maximise their revenue. He assumed an experiment with 100 houses located on a street. Two shopkeepers wish to put their shops in the best place. For the customers the best place for the shops is to have one between houses 24 and 25 and one between houses 75 and 76. In this way consumers are as close as possible on average to a shop and nobody is more than 25 houses away from a shop.

However, if the shops are competing and are more interested in maximising their own revenue than in the welfare of their customers then it is worth the shopkeeper who would otherwise have been at shop 24/25 to move towards the shopkeeper between houses 75/76: he will still keep those houses at lower numbers closer to him but he will also begin to encroach on the people closer to the shop at 75/76. The other shopkeeper will then move towards him and the stable position is that one is between 49/50 and one between 50/51. They in fact are now back in the same position of each having half of the business. But it is less convenient for the shoppers as, for instance, the person living at house No 1 or house No 100 now has to walk a long 49 houses to get their shopping, rather than just 24. The positioning of political parties is similar. They inevitably move to the centre which does not give the best representation for the voters.

As political parties pander to the floating voters to get elected, they find it increasingly difficult to discuss bad news that could upset any part of the population. They therefore have to try to be favourable to all. In particular they have to foster "growth" to try to show that they can deliver more for their citizens. There is however now ample evidence that economic growth over the last 15 years has been built on too much debt which has unwound to cause the credit crunch. It was clear to many on both sides of the Atlantic that lending someone 5 or more times their income or providing a mortgage for more than 100% of the value of a house could not be sustainable. However no politician put forward any proposals for limiting such practices, and in some cases they actually eased the regulatory burden, as to have tried to limit economic growth would have brought short term unpopularity (even though a country like France has had a 3 times income mortgage limit for many years).

There are countless other examples of when Governments have chosen the soft immediate option rather than the long-term one, ranging from failures to establish proper national infrastructure to the need to develop an agreed balance between private and public sector pension entitlements. In practice party leaders compete for the popular vote by offering competitive bribes to the electorate, often using the electorate's own money, especially in relation to state benefits.

12. The Relationship of Electors to Political Parties

Following the 2005 election the Labour pollster Philip Gould wrote about the voters:

"They felt cut out, bored, detached and disempowered. They did not believe what politicians said and did not trust their motivations. The election just watched over them, leaving them more cynical than ever. If there's one thing I would draw from this election it is this: people are switching off from politics".

Rod Liddle, BBC Editor, said in 2005:

I have never witnessed an election where there was so much disillusion and contempt shown for the people we are about to elect to govern us".

In May 2008, Matthew Parris wrote in The Times about the result of the local elections:

"There was nothing constructive in the voters' message. These elections were not an invitation to change. They were a big two-fingered salute, a raspberry, a pressing of the detrousered national buttocks to the window of the polling station. The voters are bored, tired, disillusioned and out of love."

The reasons for this political malaise have been clearly identified and stem from the contrast between people's aspirations and increasing knowledge and the arrogance of the current party political system. This has been recognised by all of the major parties but the existing oligarchical political system, where politicians with little leadership or management experience gain credibility from rising up their party's hierarchy, has proven itself unable to reform. Too many party politicians are in politics for the sake of their own career rather than for the benefits they can bring to the country and its people.

Indeed political parties have been accused of having little purpose anymore other than to provide careers for people from university politics departments! They are not focused on positive outcomes for their constituents but on gaining or maintaining power.

13. <u>The Growth of Alternative Political Mechanisms</u>

"These modern party systems reflect the exhaustion of previous main party and governing elite strategies of attempting to suppress some issues and sublimate others into a limited part of the left-right spectrum. That approach can no longer accommodate what voters want to talk about and vote about."
~ Patrick Dunleavy, political scientist

This failure of the main political system has led to the growth of pressure groups and other ways for people to express their views (90% of the public agree that if Governments do not listen, peaceful protest, blockades and demonstrations are a legitimate way of expressing people's concerns).

Independent MPs selected locally will tend to have a much closer relationship with the local community than do the current party oriented MPs. The attitude of Independent MPs is much more likely to fit in with the new style of politics in our ever changing communities.

14. <u>Conclusion</u>

The problems with the UK system can therefore be seen to be more acute than in many countries because of the confluence of issues in all four key areas of politics:

1. **Parliament:** the reduction of its ability to hold the executive to account

2. **Government:** the increase in its power but with substantial defects in its governance

3. **Parties:** the dominance of the party leadership group and the reduction in membership and importance of the local constituency associations

4. **Elections:** The shallow nature of the debate and the focus on marketing to the 2% of voters who are marginal seat targets

The UK led the world in the evolution of Parliamentary Government as society was transformed and political ideas developed. Following the huge human, technological and philosophical changes in the last 200 years since our current structures were established, the UK is now in a position to lead the world in further improving the governance of the country and the involvement of its citizens.

2D. The View of the Electorate

"A plague on both your houses"
~ Mercutio, Shakespeare

1. Turnout

The result of the 2005 general election was:

	Votes		Seats	
Labour	9,547,944	35.2%	356	55.1%
Conservative	8,772,473	32.3%	198	30.7%
LibDem	5,981,874	22.1%	62	9.6%
UKIP	612,707	2.3%	0	0.0%
SNP	412,267	1.5%	6	0.9%
Plaid Cymru	174,838	0.6%	3	0.5%
Others GB	906,665	3.3%	3	0.5%
Others NI	714,884	2.6%	18	2.8%
Total	27,123,652	100.0%	646	100.0%
Turnout:	61.3%			

Only 61.3% of the electorate actually voted at the 2005 general election. In fact, as further described below, about two-fifths voted at both the 2001 and 2005 elections, two fifths voted at one or the other, and one fifth voted at neither.

"I never vote. It only encourages them."
~ Anonymous US Voter, 1972

The loss of party loyalty and the disquiet with the current party political system are demonstrated by the abstention of the majority of voters from the electoral system as well as by the huge swings in voting behaviour which occur over specific issues. There is clear evidence that people in the UK are now ready, and indeed wanting, to vote for people of quality who are not bound by the old party system.

As it champions the issues which people in the UK really want changed in our political system the Jury Team will not only appeal to those who normally vote for the existing oligarchical parties. It will also attract many of the majority of the electorate who did not vote at both the 2001 and 2005 general elections as they saw little point in it. It may even attract back into the political system some of the estimated 7% of eligible adults who are not currently registered to vote.

2. Lack of Party Political Allegiance

The two main British political parties have had their same broad policy positions since the 1920s. For 40 years after that time political affiliation was frequently handed down through families in the same way as for religion or for support of a particular sporting team. People were able to use the party political system to simplify their decision about how to vote by relying on cues of class or job status.

Following the societal changes of the 1960s and the influence of television programmes like *That Was The Week That Was*, people's party affiliation began to weaken. Today's electorate is much more sophisticated and feels less bound by class or family ties. There is often little correlation between people's attitude on social issues and their economic background or preferences. Additionally there are now many issues which do not fit into neat party boxes and voters will support whichever party seems to them to champion their point of view.

A wide range of changes all point in the same direction of increasing voter volatility:

- voters are better educated with wider experience through television, travel and the Internet

- social and family networks have become fragmented and apply less pressure to conform

- there is less deference to authority with a greater challenge to existing structures

- economic growth means that the class issues of the 1920's are now only a part of the way in which voters evaluate parties

- the political process itself is viewed with greater suspicion

- membership of political parties has greatly reduced

- with the expansion of Government, voters see for themselves how effective or otherwise is spending on public services

In particular younger people have generally grown up in conditions of greater affluence and security than previous generations as well as having mobility and wide access to information. They believe in their right to influence their lives but are the group most disaffected from conventional politics. A 2005 survey showed that although 74% were interested in issues such as global warming, education and immigration, only 42% were at all interested in party politics.

In the mid-1960s 93% of the electorate had a clear preference for a political party and 42% identified strongly with it. By 2005 the number of strong identifiers with any political party had dropped to only 10% of the electorate.

The remaining 90% are potential floating voters. They make up their mind on the issues, which have converged between the parties, and on their immediate perceptions of the parties and their leadership. They also tend to make up their minds later during the campaigns which have themselves therefore become more important.

There is substantial evidence that voters are prepared not to vote for the traditional parties. For instance in 2005:

- a YouGov poll showed that 24% would vote for "none of the above"

- 12% of voting was for tactical reasons but as these voters were necessarily concentrated in particular seats, well over a third of the electorate in the relevant constituencies voted tactically

- only 45% of people thought that their views were properly represented by any one political party

- only 335 of the 646 constituencies had both Conservative and Labour in the top two places: in the other 311 another party came first or second

- only 41% of the electorate voted for the Conservative or Labour parties in the 2005 general election

Where there has been proportional representation the combined share of the electorate of the Conservative and Labour parties has dropped to even lower levels. Only 18% of the electorate voted for these two parties in the 2004 European Parliament Elections, only 25% at both the 2007 Scottish Parliament and Welsh Assembly Elections and only 29% in the 2008 London Assembly Elections.

There have now been twenty five local mayoral contests. Ten of these have been won by Independent candidates and they have a near-perfect re-election record. Most of them were not politicians before their initial election to mayor.

3. Volatility of Voting Intentions

The flow of the vote is very fluid. Only 38% of registered voters voted for the same party at both the 2001 and 2005 general elections. A further 21% did not vote at either election. The remaining 41% were made up as follows:

- 19% voted at one election but not the other
- 11% switched to or from the minor parties
- 7% were new voters in 2005
- only 3% switched between Conservative and Labour

Similarly of all those who voted for Labour in 2005 only 61% had voted Labour in 2001 and of those who voted Conservative in 2005 only 74% had voted Conservative in 2001.

There remains volatility within the campaign itself. The 2005 British Election Survey research showed that in their pre-election poll 46% of the electorate said that they had not yet decided how to vote. Of those who said they had decided, 18% in the end did not vote and 7% voted for another party meaning that only 35% actually voted as they expected when the campaign began. The other 65% made a decision during the campaign, changed their minds or did not vote.

MORI's 2005 survey showed that 27% of voters were still uncertain how to vote even on the day before the election.

Another example of the opportunity for substantial change in the voting result is the Green Party jumping from 0.3% of the vote in the 1987 general election to 14.9% in the 1989 European Parliament election. Similarly in 1997 Plaid Cymru gained 10% in the general election but in 1999 achieved 28% in the Welsh Assembly election. UKIP rose from 1.5% in the 2001 general election to 16.2% in the 2004 European elections.

4. Previous Campaigns

The underlying dissatisfaction with the two-party system was demonstrated as far back as 1981 by the formation of the Social Democratic Party (SDP) which subsequently allied with the Liberals. As Labour moved to the left after 1979 a number of Parliamentarians including four former Labour Cabinet Ministers

(Roy Jenkins, David Owen, Bill Rodgers and Shirley Williams) and 26 Labour MPs decided to "*break the mould*" by forming a new centre party between Labour under Michael Foot and the Conservatives who they saw as having moved to the right under Margaret Thatcher.

The "Gang of Four" said in the Limehouse Declaration that they would appeal to:

> *"those from outside politics who believe that the country cannot be saved without changing the sterile and rigid framework into which the British political system has increasingly fallen in the last two decades.*
> *We do not believe in the politics of an inert centre merely representing the lowest common denominator between two extremes. We want more, not less, radical change in our society, but with a greater stability of direction."*

Even though traditional party allegiance was much greater a quarter of a century ago than it is now, and they were dependent on conventional newspaper and broadcast media, being before the Internet, the SDP were nevertheless successful in getting more than a quarter (25.3%) of the vote in the general election of 1983. Unfortunately for them as they had wide appeal across the country, the electoral system gave them only 23 MPs whereas the Labour Party, with only 2.3% more of the vote (27.6%) but concentrated in particular areas, won 209 seats. The Alliance was similarly successful in 1987 when it won 22.5% of the vote although because of its broad based support it lost one seat to claim just 22 MPs.

Although there has not until now been a national campaign for Independent candidates, where Independents have stood on special issues they have demonstrated that a large proportion of the electorate will vote for them. For instance in the last three general elections:

- In 1997 Martin Bell stood as an Independent candidate in Tatton, one of the safest Conservative seats in the country, with only a 24 day campaign from when he resigned from the BBC. He overturned the majority of over 20,000 of the sitting Conservative Member of Parliament, Neil Hamilton, who was embroiled in "sleaze" allegations, and Bell was elected an MP with a majority of 11,077 votes and 60.2% of the votes

- In 2001 Dr Richard Taylor stood in Wyre Forest in protest at the closure of the local accident and emergency unit. He won in 2001 with a majority of over 18,000 and 58.1% of the vote and won again in 2005

- In 2005 Peter Law, a member of the Welsh Assembly, resigned from the Labour Party in protest at an all women shortlist being imposed in Blaenau Gwent and beat the official Labour candidate. Labour had enjoyed a majority of 19,313, making it the safest Parliamentary seat in Wales, but Law won the seat with a majority of 9,121 and 58.2% of the vote

This voter volatility is a trend throughout the western democracies. For instance Ross Perot gained 19% of the US Presidential vote in 1992 and in Europe instant parties such as Berlusconi's Forza Italia, Jorg Haider's Freedom Party in Austria and List Pym Fortuyn in the Netherlands all show the increased volatility of the electorate.

Chapter 3

THE JURY TEAM

"It's amazing what we can accomplish when nobody cares who gets the credit."

1. The Philosophy of Independent Candidates

The social changes and technology which have led to the centralisation of political power have now developed to the extent that they can fulfill Newton's Third Law that "*every action has an equal and opposite reaction*".

People have become empowered by communication and by the availability of information. These trends provide the opportunity to remove the representation of the people by oligarchical political parties and reinstate that representation by people of independent integrity and goodwill.

Independent candidates such as Martin Bell, Richard Taylor and Peter Law have shown that Independents can be elected as MPs even if they operate alone with no national representation. The Jury Team will be able to provide a national platform and publicity for all of its candidates.

The Jury Team will bring back the independence of MPs, MEPs, councillors and members of devolved governments so that they are no longer beholden to a party political machine. The Jury Team will allow voters to go back to being able to choose a person who they believe will best serve their country. As the 18th Century political philosopher John Stuart Mill said about electors:

The End Of The Party

"His vote is not a thing in which he has an option. He is bound to give it according to his best and his most conscientious opinion of the public good. The voter is under an absolute moral obligation to consider the interest of the public, not his private advantage, and give his vote to the best of his judgment exactly as he would be bound to do if he were the sole voter and the election depended upon him alone."

The Jury Team MEPs, MPs and other elected representatives will not be bound by a whipping system and will be there to represent the interests of the country and of their constituents rather than an oligarchical party political leadership.

"Representative Government is no longer as compelling a proposition as it once was. Instead, a search for new institutional forms to express conflicts of interest has begun."
~ Professor Ralf Dahrendorf

Support for the Jury Team Governance Principles will mean that the new style of Jury Team representatives are independent, paid appropriately, agree to term limits and an independent politicians complaints procedure, promote citizen-inspired referendums and operate a sensible system of departmental Government with independent statistics showing the effect of Government policies. The Jury Team requires commitment to no discrimination.

This right of representatives of the people to be independent is properly protected in many other jurisdictions. In particular Rule 2 of the European Parliament, building on the experience of continental legislatures, states:

Rule 2: The independent mandate: Members of the European Parliament shall exercise their mandate independently. They shall not be bound by any instructions and shall not receive a binding mandate.

Similar issues exist with local and devolved government. A letter from Councillor George Ashcroft in the magazine TotalPolitics said:

"I was very interested to read Phil Hendren's analysis of the Orange report on the future of politics (TP, February). I quite agree that the political party of the future needs to change. I was

elected as a Conservative councillor in 2007 and since that time have been subject to a group whip on a number of occasions.

I have come to believe that this system is abused by those who seek to stifle debate and dissention, across all parties. Recently, I defied the whip and was promptly sacked from my cabinet assistant position, leading to my departure from the Conservative Party.

At just turned 31, I am a relatively young councillor and I suspect that many other young people are completely unaccustomed to voting contrary to their conscience. Involvement with party politics will come as a rude awakening to them.
I have never cared for being told how to vote on any issue and quite frankly, in the age of the internet and individual protest, neither should I expect to be."

2. The Key Tasks for the Jury Team

Computer and mobile phone technology has now made it possible for people to choose a coherent national group of independent candidates to be MEPs or MPs. The Jury Team has identified the following requirements for its success:

- The relevance and reach of the Internet and mobile phone technology amongst those interested in political issues in the UK

- The successful development of the juryteam.org website and of the integrated mobile telephone technology

- People believing that they can make a difference by nominating themselves as Jury Team candidates to be MEPs or MPs

- The general public voting in sufficient numbers for the selection of the Jury Team candidates to be credible for the European, Westminster or other elections

- The election of the Jury Team candidates against the representatives of the traditional political parties

Each of these five stages is addressed below.

3. The Reach of Internet and Mobile Phone Technology

Writing in The Times in September 2008, Dan Sabbagh said:

"Anybody who can think ahead to the next election ought to appreciate that there are longer-term media trends that should - if used properly - change the face of politics next time round.

It is worth remembering that YouTube did not exist during the last election (it was launched in December 2005), that social networking was not in anybody's consciousness and the broadband penetration that makes internet video possible has roughly doubled from 30 per cent to 60 per cent."

In an article in The Financial Times in October 2008, John Lloyd commented:

"If the screen is to be our window on democracy, can we merge the new and the old, the voting slip with the mouse click?

If the screen, whether of a television or of a computer (and the two will soon be one), is to be our window on the world of democratic as well as consumer and entertainment choice, then is it possible to marry the old but still existent with the new and now emerging? To merge Wikis with Westminster or Washington, the voting slip with the mouse click?

It is clear that the public sphere is increasingly being evacuated for lack of interest; but on the screens that flicker behind curtains and shutters, in the private sphere, judgments can be made based on observable character traits, can be calibrated with what one knows about human nature, can be free of the complexity and tedium of governance and public life."

Nielsen Online estimate that in September 2008 there were 28.2 million Active Home Internet Users in the UK. A further 6.9 million people are Active Users of the Internet at work. This gives a total of 35.1 million people who actively accessed the Internet during September 2008. In addition there are a further 6.8 million people who have access to the Internet at home or work but who did not access it during September 2008, a total with access of 41.9 million. This number includes those under 18 but it is nevertheless a substantial proportion of the 45 million registered voters making up the UK electorate.

The 35.1 million people who accessed the web during September 2008 on average did so in 45 separate sessions and viewed 81 web domains. They spent an average of 69 minutes on each session leading to total browsing time of 51 hours and 55 minutes during the month, an average of over 1 hour 40 minutes per day. 30.4 million people accessed a Google website, 27.4 million Microsoft, and around 18 million for each of Yahoo!, BBC and eBay.

During 2008 the market research company TNS conducted a survey of internet usage, *Digital World, Digital Life*, based on over 27,000 interviews in 16 countries. This found that the UK population on average spend 28% of their leisure time on the net. The survey found that British housewives spend almost half of their free time (47%) on the net, over 2 hours 40 minutes per day, despite having just 5.8 free hours on a weekday, barely above the UK average of 5.2 hours. Students spent 39% and the unemployed 32% of their leisure time on the net. The study also found that many traditional activities are now being done online. Three-quarters of Britons have used the internet for banking in the past month and the same proportion had read news online in the past month. Two-thirds had paid bills online and 62% had checked the weather.

The British population is well accustomed to voting with their mobile phones. According to Ofcom, in 2008 there were 122.6 active mobile phone connections for every 100 people. 92% of households have a mobile phone. Ofcom also states that only 25% of adults never use text messaging, compared to 28% who never use the internet. These usage rates are clearly much higher than the 60% who vote at general elections or 39% at European elections.

A survey of 2,136 British adults conducted by YouGov after the 2005 general election suggests that two-thirds of people who did not vote would be more likely to vote if online voting is available. This mirrors previous research by the Electoral Commission. A Qire survey of 3,000 Londoners in April 2008 found that 26% of respondents would be willing to vote in the London Mayor election using mobile phones. This builds on the use of mobile voting in reality and other TV shows where, famously, more people, especially the younger generation, cast votes for Big Brother in 2005 than in that year's general election.

4. The juryteam.org Website and Mobile Telephone Technology

The Jury Team has registered not only the juryteam.org website but also the similar websites which people might access such as juryteam.com, juryteam.biz, juryteam.info, juryteam.mobi, juryteam.tv, juryteam.me, juryteam.eu, juryteam.co.uk and juryteam.org.uk. Anyone accessing these other sites will be automatically directed to the juryteam.org website.

The website and the mobile phone technology will be integrated so that people looking at the website can immediately vote for the candidate they wish to support.

Voting will begin as soon as candidates are registered on the website. People will vote by mobile phone for their choice(s) from all of the potential candidates who have put their name forward.

Once the primary voting period has finished towards the end of April, the successful candidates will be required to attend a meeting with Jury Team representatives to check their credentials. In the event that any candidate does not meet the necessary criteria of nationality or is unable to confirm their educational or career history then the next person in terms of votes received will be chosen. Candidates will also be given training.

Advertisements in regional and national newspapers can be used to ensure that the electorate are aware of the potential candidates and are encouraged to vote for them by mobile phone.

A version of this process for a primary election was used in 2008 in the London Borough of Newham for the election of a Young Mayor. Sixty individuals aged up to 18 put themselves forward and 15 were selected in a primary web voting process as shown on http://www.newham.gov.uk/YoungMayor/Elections/PrimaryElectionArchive2008.htm.

In order to vote for their selected candidate(s), people will go to the juryteam.org website where they will be able to look at all of the potential Jury Team candidates in their region (MEP) or constituency (MP) and decide who they wish to vote for. These lists will show summary details (which can be clicked on to go to the full nomination form) and will be sortable by name, by postcode and by the policy areas in which the candidate is interested. Each potential candidate will be asked to select a "candidate code" to identify themselves, e.g. janesmith01 (a minimum of five and a maximum of eight letters plus two numbers).

When people have made their choice of who they wish to select as their Jury Team candidate they will be asked to use their mobile phone to send a message to the short code 86837. On a standard mobile phone this spells VOTER. When the message is sent the person sending it will put in the name of the candidate they wish to vote for, e.g. janesmith01. They will then immediately be sent a message back to inform them that the candidate code was a valid vote and asking them to opt in to receive further communications via email or phone. In the event that the candidate code submitted has been misspelled or for some other reason does not exist the voter will be notified and asked to vote again.

Only UK registered SIM cards will be accepted. Unlike TV talent shows, where each SIM card is allowed multiple votes for the same person, the Jury Team will allow each SIM card to vote only once for each candidate. This leads to "one phone, one vote per candidate".

If people do vote again for the same candidate then the vote will be ignored and they will be sent an error message. People may perhaps wish to vote for more than one candidate as a group of candidates may share the person's political priorities. It will therefore be valid to vote from one phone for more than one candidate. People will also be able to remove a vote if they change their mind by sending a message to VOTER with the phrase "Not" janesmith01 which will then cancel any vote for janesmith01 that has been cast by that phone.

People may well ask their friends to vote for them as a candidate which is entirely legitimate. This will require their friends to send in a message to VOTER with the candidate code of the person they wish to vote for. Their SIM card will be registered.

Voters will be charged a 25 pence fee which will cover the cost of the return messages to be sent to them and of the website administration.

The candidates selected in the primaries through the above process to represent the Jury Team will stand in the actual elections as the candidates for the Jury Team in the same way as do candidates for the traditional parties. The Jury Team candidates will be among the choices on the official ballot paper

5. The Nomination Form

The Nomination Form to become a Jury Team potential candidate for the Westminster election is shown in Appendix 2 and the one for the European Parliament is essentially similar but with Constituency replaced by Region and minor legal changes. The Forms are designed to encourage people to set out their real achievements and reasons for wanting to become MPs or MEPs. They invite candidates to describe their background, their reason for wanting to be selected in the particular constituency or region and their interest in up to three of the policy areas with which Government is concerned.

In order to ensure that no fascist or similarly extreme people can be considered for selection, the form also requires all candidates to confirm that they agree not to support any policies discriminating on the basis of race, colour, gender, sexual orientation, disability or religious or other belief. Similarly all candidates will have to agree to adhere to the Nolan Principles of Public Life: Selflessness, Integrity, Objectivity, Accountability, Openness, Honesty and Leadership.

Candidates will have to state the region or constituency for which they wish to be selected (but may propose themselves in separate applications in more than one region or constituency if they believe that they have suitable local credentials).

The form requires a Proposer and Seconder to be named and confirmation of the accuracy of the application. There will be a fee of £25 to cover the costs of the application and the materials, including this book, that will be sent to all registered candidates (this will also deter frivolous applications).

When submitted, the Nomination Form will be manually reviewed by a member of the Jury Team staff to ensure that it does not contain any offensive or suspect material. Once approved, which will normally occur within 24 hours, the Nomination Form will be posted on the website and the mobile voting for that candidate will be simultaneously activated. (If a Nomination Form is rejected then the candidate will be notified by email).

Candidates will in addition be recommended to use the MySpace, Facebook and similar social networking web communities and other sites such as Twitter and YouTube in order to give themselves the maximum coverage on the web.

6. Jury Team Candidates

It is expected that many people respected in their community will submit their names as Jury Team candidates. For instance in the survey of how well different professions are trusted (in which MPs and ministers score only 27% and 24% respectively) family doctors scored 92%, head teachers 84% and senior police officers 68%. Candidates will have many different backgrounds, for instance including charity workers, sports stars, managers, former members of the civil service or armed forces, artists or research scientists. There are also likely to be a number of candidates from the over 2,000 Independent councillors in the UK who represent around 10% of all councillors.

A letter from John Allison of Maidenhead to The Times in January 2009 about who might join Parliament said:

"I would like people from the Royal Society, the engineering institutions, architects, farmers, fishermen, local businesses, the medical profession and other bodies that can offer specialist knowledge and experience not likely to be found in the public and political sectors."

There is plenty of evidence that a considerable number of candidates will put themselves forward. Many people do not wish currently to be political candidates because they want to be able to use their judgment when elected and not be whipped as part of a party machine.

At local level a survey organised by Ipsos/MORI and the Standards Board for England investigated what would lead people to become candidates as local councillors. In answer to the question *"I am now going to read out a list of factors which might encourage people to stand as a local councillor, and I would like you to tell me which one of the following applies to you. You may choose up to three factors."*, half of Londoners said they would be encouraged to stand as a councillor if they thought they could make a difference:

Feeling I could make a difference	**50%**
Having more info about what was involved	34%
Having more spare time	28%
Knowing I would be paid regular income	24%
If politicians had a better reputation	20%

Those mentioning two or three things were then asked *"Of the two or three factors you mentioned, which one would most encourage you to stand as a local councillor?"*. There was even more relative support for standing if people felt that they *"could make a difference"*.

Feeling I could make a difference	**45%**
Having more info about what was involved	16%
Having more spare time	12%
Knowing I would be paid regular income	10%
If politicians had a better reputation	7%

It therefore seems very clear that if people think they *"could make a difference"* then they will be prepared to stand, especially as the Jury Team will provide assistance in moving towards public office.

The Jury Team will widely publicise the opportunity to stand as a candidate. All major membership associations and organisations like the Local Government Association Independent Group of councillors, charities, community groups, business associations, self-help groups, and similar bodies will be contacted to ask them to encourage their members to participate.

7. Public Interest in Selecting the Jury Team candidate

The Jury Team process itself should greatly increase interest in politics. People will realise that every vote will count and that they now have the opportunity directly to select the person who can represent them.

Huge numbers of people vote using their mobile phones for contests on television and in the newspapers:

- 16.5 million text votes cast during the last series of *X-Factor*

- 6.8 million text votes cast in the final week of *Big Brother*

- 1.5 million text votes cast during the evening of the *Dancing on Ice* finale

With that potential involvement and the associated publicity there is every likelihood that the chosen candidates will succeed at the election itself. Independent politicians are more likely to be trusted than those who are just part of a distant party machine.

8. Jury Team Candidates – European Parliament

The European elections have from 3 to 10 seats in each of the twelve electoral regions with one region for each of Scotland, Wales and Northern Ireland and nine for England. The Jury Team will field 69 candidates, one for each seat, in each region in England, Scotland and Wales where the party list system operates. In Northern Ireland, with the Single Transferable Vote system, it only makes sense to field one candidate. This leads to a national total of 70 candidates.

The juryteam.org website will include a section setting out the background to being an MEP, of which there are 785 across the European Union. They are elected once every five years by voters in the 27 member States on behalf of its 492 million citizens.

An MEP has explained the benefits of the office as:

"Being an MEP opens doors. It provides access to ministers of the Crown in Britain, to the British establishment, to the people who run businesses and daily make decisions that affect millions of other people. As a member of the public I get fobbed off with responses from flunkeys, as we all are. As an MEP I get responses

from the ministers and chief executives who address the issues I've raised. I can now take the concerns of ordinary people into boardrooms and ministerial offices as never before, and have them taken seriously.

Being an MEP gives me access to information. I now have a research team in Brussels and here in the UK paid for by the EU, would you believe, who are able to dig into the detail of EU regulations, directives and future plans. We have access to the EU's library, its databases and officials."

The juryteam.org website will also set out the basic role of MEPs which the European Parliament describes as:

"Parliament plays an active role in drafting legislation which has an impact on the daily lives of its citizens: for example, on environmental protection, consumer rights, equal opportunities, transport, and the free movement of workers, capital, services and goods. In addition to their growing role as legislators, MEPs approve the appointment of the European Commission, decide the EU budget with the member states, monitor spending, approve international agreements, question EU Commissioners and national Ministers, and appoint the European Ombudsman.

The European Parliament's budget for the year 2007 was €1,397 million. This covers staff costs, buildings, MEPs' travel allowance and expenses. The Parliament employs about 5,900 people, of whom about 1,300 work in the linguistic services covering 23 working languages."

Salaries of MEPs are the same as national MPs in their own countries: UK MEPs and MPs currently earn £ 63,291 per year but this is planned to increase substantially from July 2009 with the implementation of a standard EU-wide salary for MEPs. MEPs also receive generous travel, office and attendance allowances.

The European Parliament election is being held in the UK on the 4th June 2009 (7am - 10pm). The Notice of Election must be published not later than Tuesday 28th April and nomination papers may be submitted from the date to be stated on the Notice of Election until 4pm on Thursday 7th May.

The timetable for the selection of Jury Team candidates will therefore be:

- Launch of the Jury Team in mid March

- Candidates invited to submit their applications from mid March

- Voting for candidates starts in mid March and lasts for six weeks

9. Jury Team Candidates – Westminster Parliament

At the Westminster elections, which use the first past the post system, the Jury Team will put forward one candidate in each of the 650 new Parliamentary constituencies (increased from the 646 in the 2005 general election)..

The precise timetable for selection will depend on the expected timing of the election as described in Chapter 1 but it will follow the same pattern as for the European Parliament election as set out above.

The arithmetic of voting helps the Jury Team which will appeal across traditional party boundaries. There is every reason why someone to the left, in the middle or to the right of traditional groupings would wish to vote for better governance.

For a first-past-the-post election, if the Jury Team draws votes uniformly from all other parties then the proportion of votes it needs to obtain to win is significantly lower than was achieved by the previous winning candidate (assuming no other changes). This is illustrated in the table below (%):

Share of Previous Winner	Jury Team Takes	New Share of Previous Winner
30.0	23.2	23.0
35.0	26.0	25.9
40.0	28.7	28.5
45.0	31.1	31.0
50.0	33.4	33.3
55.0	35.6	35.4
60.0	37.6	37.4
65.0	39.5	39.3

Thus, as an example, if the current MP won the seat with 40% and the Jury Team takes 28.7% of the vote from the incumbent and from the other parties, then the incumbent's share will be reduced to 28.5% which means that the Jury Team would win the seat (subject to no other changes).

The number of seats in each category of the share of vote won by the current incumbent in the 2005 general election is set out in the following table. This shows in the first column a range of the percentage of the votes cast obtained by the winning candidate and in the second column the number of seats with an incumbent's winning share in that range:

Vote (%)	Number of Seats
60+	36
55-60	55
50-55	129
45-50	208
40-45	162
35-40	46
30-35	10
	646

It can be seen that 56 seats were won with a share of vote of less than 40%. On the formula shown above, this means that the Jury

Team would have to gain a share of vote of about 28.7% to win all of these seats. A further 162 seats have shares of votes of 40% to 45% and these would require the Jury Team to have uniform support from 28.7% to 31.1% of the electorate. A further 208 seats would be gained if support achieved 33.4%.

The mid-point of the 646 seats at number 323 is a share of vote of 47.3% which would require Jury Team support of 32.1% of the electorate.

This analysis therefore shows that if the Jury Team could achieve one-third of the votes of the electorate from across the political spectrum then it could gain the majority of the seats in the House of Commons. This requirement is not much more than the SDP achieved a quarter of a century ago when party loyalty was much greater, and politicians held in greater respect, and very much less than the 58-60% achieved by the last three Independent MPs to be elected to Westminster.

The Jury Team anticipates having substantial influence in the next Parliament. The expected outcome of the next general election for ranges of swing in the national vote for just Labour and the Conservatives have been calculated by the academic election experts Colin Rallings and Michael Thrasher as follows:

Uniform national swing	**Result**
Any to Lab	Increased Labour majority in Parliament
Up to 1.6% to Con	Reduced Labour majority
1.6% - 4.3% to Con	Labour run hung parliament (A Conservative lead of up to 6%)
4.3% - 6.9% Con	Conservative run hung parliament (A Conservative lead of up to 9%)
More than 6.9% to Con	Conservative overall majority (A Conservative lead of over 9%)

This demonstrates the likelihood of a hung Parliament if the Conservatives have a lead, as they have had for much of the current Parliament, of anywhere from 3 to 9%. The Jury Team would be able to achieve a considerable positive effect on legislation and governance in any of these swing scenarios.

10. Administration of the Jury Team

The Jury Team is registering with the Electoral Commission as a political party as required by law. A senior Party Council is being set up of men and women from around the UK to give assurance to voters that the Jury Team will be properly run. This will however be purely administrative and will not indulge in any policy advice other than in relation to governance.

One area which has brought the political parties particularly into disrepute has been party funding. The Jury Team will encourage small individual donations through its website. This money will be used to support individual candidates and the national campaign.

As well as coordinating the technology required to achieve the selection of candidates outside the restrictions of current political parties, the Jury Team will also be able to help its candidates with:

- the administrative and legal requirements to register as a candidate

- a forum of best practice on campaigning and fundraising

- research showing the key governance issues of importance to voters

- financial support to the campaigns of candidates selected for the Jury Team

The Jury Team will therefore ensure that the electorate are aware that its candidates are independent with strong adherence to better governance and that all of their donations will be properly used.

Governance

THE TWELVE JURY TEAM PROPOSALS

A. Letting MPs be Independent

"Some men change their party for the sake of their principles; others their principles for the sake of their party"
~ Winston Churchill

1. History of Parliamentary Development

In Chapter 2B the development of Parliament and Government was described. The battles fought by the British people over the centuries were to bring the monarchs and their Privy Councils under the scrutiny of Parliament. Following the Glorious Revolution of 1688, by the time of the accession of George III in 1760 this principle had been largely won.

Parliament was designed to debate and as appropriate agree or disagree with the proposals of the monarch and his or her ministers. .The ministers then oversaw the implementation of the agreed legislation by collecting taxes, organizing collective activities such as armies or construction projects and ensuring the administration of the law.

Parliament was based on individuals in the legislature being representatives of their constituencies who could challenge and determine the correctness of the proposals of the monarch and ministers. MPs had the freedom to vote as they saw best in all the circumstances. In his 1774 Letter to the Electors of Bristol, Edmund Burke stated about MPs:

"His unbiased opinion, his mature judgment, his enlightened conscience, he ought not to sacrifice to you or to any set of men living."

2. The Contrasting Current Position

Nowadays of course Members of Parliament almost entirely do sacrifice their judgment to *"any set of men living",* they being the party to which they belong. It is very rare for any Government to suffer any defeat in the House of Commons and indeed the current Labour Government suffered no such policy defeat throughout its first two terms from 1997-2005 when it enacted much contentious legislation. MPs were characterised as early as 1946 by the Conservative MP Christopher Hollis:

"On most votes it would be simpler and more economic to keep a flock of tame sheep and from time to time to drive them through the division lobbies in the appropriate numbers".

MPs are corralled, with the graphic word "whipped" being used to describe the process, to vote in line with the wishes of their party leadership. They often vote for a motion with only the very slightest idea of what it entails. This is evidenced from those MPs who are not attending a debate, usually over 80% of the total, but are at another meeting within the Division Bell area who have to rush to vote. They will often admit that they have little idea about the substance of the motion on which they are voting. Almost all of what is approved by Parliament is now just a rubber stamp of what has been decided by a Government department.

In November 2005, Roy Hattersley, the former Labour Party Deputy Leader, wrote in The Times:

"Labour backbenchers — the most supine Members of Parliament in British history — must decide where their loyalty lies."

In 2007 the Labour MP Alan Simpson announced that he would be resigning at the next general election. In his resignation letter to his Nottingham South constituency he said:

"I never went into Parliament to have a career. I went in to change the world. I'm leaving because I still want to change the world, and I don't think you can do that in this Parliament. My worry is that it has become a comfort zone in which MPs are paid more and more to stand for less and less. There are good people in the Parliamentary Labour Party; just not enough of them. Many MPs complain of a Government that no longer listens to the party, but they dutifully walk through the division lobbies to vote for whatever regressive measures Downing Street asks for. At times I feel that colleagues would vote for the slaughter of the first-born if asked to."

In October 2008, Simon Jenkins wrote in The Sunday Times:

"In all my years of writing this column, from which I am standing down, I have been amazed at the spinelessness of Britain's elected representatives in defending liberty and protesting against state arrogance. They appear as parties to the conspiracy of power. There have been outspoken judges, outspoken peers, even outspoken journalists. There have been few outspoken MPs. Those supposedly defending freedom are whipped into obedience."

3. The Effect of Unfettered Government Legislation

One of the key advantages of the concept of independent MPs is that it would ensure better scrutiny of legislation and regulation.

The volume of legislation has grown hugely with there now being about 8 new laws or regulations a day. According to Sweet & Maxwell, the legal publishers, in Margaret Thatcher's time as Prime Minister there were an average of 1,724 pieces of legislation per year. Under Tony Blair this increased by over a half to 2,663 laws per year. Gordon Brown's first year saw a further 6% increase to 2,823 new laws (64% more than the figure for Thatcher) despite his repeated pledges to cut down on the amount of red tape with which businesses and other organisations have to comply.

The "bible" for tax experts is Tolleys Yellow Tax Handbook. This contained 4,555 pages in 1997 but this has now more than doubled to 9,841 pages. A similar example of massive legislative activity is in the area of the Home Office where in the five years since 2003 there have been five new Criminal Justice Acts, a total of 910 sections and 104 schedules. Across all departments, 1,036 new criminal offences have been enacted since 1997.

In February 2009, Richard Thomas, the Information Commissioner, was reported in The Times as criticising proposals going through parliament to allow mass data sharing between government departments and the private sector. He said that other key government surveillance measures had been "pushed through" without proper scrutiny or parliamentary debate.

In the same month, Sir Ken Macdonald, Director of Public Prosecutions from 2003-08, wrote in The Times:

"In Britain we had an additional burden: legislators who preferred criminal justice to be an auction of fake toughness, so long as the toughness was not too tough to design. So no one likes terrorists? Let's bring in lots of terror laws, the tougher the better. Let's lock up nasty people longer, and for longer before they are charged. Let's stop medieval clerics winding up the tabloids. Let's stop off-colour comedians outraging homophobic preachers. Let's pretend that outlawing offensiveness makes the world less offensive.

This frequently made useful headlines. But it didn't make our country or any other country a better or safer place to live. It didn't respect our way of life. It brought us the War on Terror and it didn't make it any easier for us to progress into the future with comfort and security.

Our legislators faltered because they seemed to ignore the fact that what makes good politics doesn't always make good policy. And they didn't want to tackle the more complex issues that really affect safety in people's lives. It was easier to throw increasingly illiberal sound bites at a shadowy and fearsome enemy."

The Sixth Report on *The British Regulatory System* published by the British Chambers of Commerce stated:

"Despite expressed concern with the total volume of regulation, their pace of introduction, as measured by (R)IAs, has continued to increase. About 130 regulations per annum were generated in the first four years of this Government. The number has increased progressively to about 350 in the year covered by this report, the year to 30th June 2007. The cumulative burden on British

business since 1998 is, according to the (R)IAs themselves, £66bn., of which 70 per cent arises from EU sourced regulation (73 per cent last year). In terms of the number of regulations, the EU accounts for only about 35 per cent."

The Association of Chartered Certified Accountants has stated that: *"The cost of complying with red tape can be proportionally up to 30 times higher for SMEs (small and medium sized enterprises) than for larger firms"*

Jeremy Clarkson expressed a popular resentment about the tide of regulation when he wrote in The Sunday Times in June 2008:

"The machine needs to be fed. When you have 650 members of parliament elected to make laws, and an army of 500,000 civil servants whose job is to make sure that those laws work, and more legions in Brussels making more laws, there is never going to be any respite. The machine can never rest until absolutely everything is illegal.

Whenever I let my mind wander, I become quivery-lipped and frightened thinking about all the things I could do 10 years ago that I cannot do now. I may not smack my children, for instance, or talk on a mobile telephone while driving or put too much salt on my mashed potato or smoke at home if my cleaning lady objects or give my donkey a tender burial or encourage my dogs to kill rats. And if I put the wrong thing in the wrong-coloured dustbin, I'm likely to spend the next five years digging tunnels."

Governments since the 1980s have said how they want to reduce regulatory burdens but they have clearly failed. Businesses, charities, national and local public authorities and other employers are somehow supposed to read, assimilate and implement a barrage of new regulations, which may have some individual validity, but which the current system of minimal Parliamentary scrutiny allows to be introduced at far too great a rate. Employer related regulations are now normally implemented at specific times such as the beginning of the tax year which means that the magnitude of the new employer requirements can be clearly seen. In the first week of April 2008, the Government implemented 128 new statutes and statutory instruments affecting employers, covering thousands of pages, a 58% increase on the 81 that came into force on the same date in 2007. The April 2008 ones included significant pieces of legislation requiring detailed study and often substantial management time such as:

- The introduction of the Corporate Manslaughter Act
- Changes to the Sex Discrimination Act in relation to pregnancy, maternity leave and harassment
- The extension of the Occupational Pensions Schemes regulations: organisations with more than 50 employees must consult with members of pension schemes before making changes to future pensions arrangements
- New Employment Equality regulations relating to employee benefits based on the length of service
- New provisions for employment agencies to protect the rights of agency workers

These provisions, possibly valid individually, nevertheless swamp organisations with bureaucracy which leads to fewer jobs. Government has produced no cost/benefit analysis of the total effect of the new regulations that are annually or more frequently introduced.

4. The Effects of the Party Political System

In Westminster the reputation and effectiveness of the "Mother of Parliaments" have become perverted by the reinforcing effect of strong political parties and the power of Prime Ministers. Parliament no longer satisfies the electorate nor oversees a system of Government which allows the UK to be competitive in the 21st century.

George Washington foresaw the problems which would arise if parties were allowed to develop when he wrote in his Farewell Address in 1796:

"I have already intimated to you the danger of parties in the state ... The alternate domination of one faction over another, sharpened by the spirit of revenge, natural to party dissension, which in different ages and countries has perpetrated the most horrid enormities, is itself a frightful despotism.

The End Of The Party

The common and continual mischiefs of the spirit of party are sufficient to make it the interest and duty of a wise people to discourage and restrain it."

Ray Mallon, elected independent Mayor of Middlesborough, has said:

"I do feel the party system is detrimental if it results in politicians paying more attention to the whip than the real needs of the people they represent"

Political parties have nevertheless grown and now prevail in our political system. Consequently the voting choices of MPs are dominated by their being just delegates of their political party, often described as "lobby fodder". Parliament is in disrepute because its traditional scrutiny role has been taken away and it only rarely provides any serious challenge to the authority of the executive. The growth in:

- the strength of the central political party organisations and whipping system

- the number of Westminster Village MPs whose career depends on party patronage, and

- the power of the party leaders to dominate policy development

have all led to individual MPs having almost no opportunity to make their views count through their primary functions of scrutiny and voting.

5. <u>The Political Class</u>

Historically most MPs had had a successful previous occupation before coming into Parliament and even a generation ago MPs represented a wide range of backgrounds and skills. However nowadays they are often career politicians who, from after leaving college, have lived and worked in the Westminster Village.

As they have to select a political party when they set out on their career their entire success is dependent on promotion by their chosen party. Getting to the *"top of the greasy pole"* as described by Disraeli. They therefore have to be obedient and find themselves not allowed to express their true feelings if they wish to progress. The benefit for them is that if they are loyal they will be promoted and the party label will help to protect them from personal responsibility.

Peter Oborne now estimates that the Political Class comprises about 5,000 people across the whole of the UK including elected members, party officials and political correspondents.

A survey undertaken as part of the international RACATEL project (Raising Civil Awareness Through English language), conducted in the UK by the Workers Educational Association of Sheffield found:

> *"Whilst no-one in the UK group felt that politicians (local or national) were corrupt, they did feel that politics attracted the worst sort of person: egotistical, opportunistic and morally light weight. They felt that high office often led to self aggrandisement and felt offended by the casual picking up of additional payments from the media and advisory roles with corporations."*

6. The Party Policy Agenda

This regimentation of MPs is completely contrary to the principles of Parliament whose very name means (from the French *parler*) a place to speak and discuss. In normal life a group of people will find themselves agreeing about some matters and disagreeing about others. Nobody would ever normally accept all of the views of another person or entity.

The main political parties have had to become wide coalitions. The Conservative Party includes those who are for economic and personal freedom (Libertarians), those for economic freedom but with clear moral views (Thatcherites) and those who wish the state both to intervene and to restrict moral choices (One-Nation in the Macmillan heritage). Similarly Labour has been torn between Old Labour and New Labour with different views about the effectiveness of markets and how strong should be the "nanny state". The Liberal Democrats have supported policies from allowing prisoners to vote to greater state intervention to tax cuts.

Even many party members therefore agree with only some of the policies of their party at any one time and will often vociferously disagree on others. This richness of view is entirely proper in a democracy. US President Herbert Hoover recognised that real life issues need discussion as widely as possible when he said:

"Honest differences of views and honest debate are not disunity. They are the vital process of policymaking among free men."

7. <u>Free Votes</u>

Party leaderships used to give their members more opportunities for free votes. In 1971 Edward Heath initially insisted that the vote on the paving motion on the principle of entry to the EEC should be subject to a three-line whip. This had the effect of provoking Conservative dissidents to press for a free vote so that they could oppose entry without being disloyal to the party. Just before the First Reading vote on the Bill in October 1971 the Government declared that there was to be a free vote as the issue was a matter of conscience. Most Conservatives voted for membership, but 39 voted against and two abstained. There was a Labour three-line whip instructing Members to oppose UK entry, but 69 pro-European Labour MPs voted in favour of entry and 20 abstained.

Free votes are now very much restricted. The only key area where MPs are still allowed to make their own decisions, other than on matters of conscience, is on the very limited number of private members' bills. These have dropped from an average of 17 successful ones per year in the 1960s to just 3 in 2005-6 and 4 in 2006-7, another erosion of the discretion of backbench MPs.

Conscience issues include areas such as embryo research, sexual orientation, euthanasia and capital punishment. These are very difficult societal issues which none of the political parties wishes formally to address but it is instructive to see how by allowing a free vote a decision can be reached which is accepted by the population at large.

There are nevertheless continual party leadership attempts to try to reduce even this freedom for MPs as evidenced by the Government's attitude to whipping and Parliamentary procedure for the 2008 Human Fertilisation and Embryology Bill. MPs on both sides of the issue accused the Government of *"bringing Parliament into disrepute"* for allowing only four three-hour debates. The Government also initially insisted on a whipped vote at Second Reading and only backed down when faced by the pressure of resignation from three Roman Catholic ministers. It did however continue to insist on a whipped vote at Third Reading and as a result Ruth Kelly, the Transport Secretary, was visibly absent for the vote.

There is clearly no democratic justification for matters of equal or greater significance to the British population being whipped when some directly of interest to only a minority of people can be given a free vote.

Legislation about going to war, establishing major new Government agencies, increasing Government intervention in the economy or in an individual's private life, deciding on how personal or corporate income should be redistributed through the taxation system and a vast number of other legislative and regulatory proposals are also ones which directly impact on the lives of UK citizens as much as or indeed more than those on which a free vote is allowed.

In contrast to the current whipped, and therefore minimal, legislative process, all of these matters would benefit from a free and fair discussion in the House of Commons. There is a strong argument for less but better legislation. Unfortunately the whipping system does not allow any substantive or effective debate.

8. The Effectiveness of the Opposition Party

It is sometimes said that the Government is held to account by the Opposition. However although the Opposition does have access to the media and can express its views there, by definition it does not have the votes in the Commons either to cause Government actually to change its policies or to win a censure motion. The increasingly partisan nature of Parliament, not least in the yah-boo politics of Prime Minister's Questions, means that the opportunities for compromise have also become less. Much of the Parliamentary and other political debate is staged largely for the benefit of the television cameras.

The practical problems that this brings were discussed in July 2008 in an article by Sean O'Neill, Crime Editor of The Times. He described comments made by Deputy Assistant Commissioner Alf

Hitchcock who was chosen by Jacqui Smith, the Home Secretary, to develop a plan for fighting knife crime in eight hotspot areas of the country:

"As the Home Secretary's ideas were derided as "half-baked" and "piecemeal" by opposition spokesmen, Mr Hitchcock called for a united front by politicians to tackle the problem. He said: "One of the worries I have is the way that this issue is being used politically at the moment. This is a time for the parties to stop using it as a political argument and to start working together. I'm sure there are good ideas in Government and good ideas in the Opposition and drawing these ideas together would be better than fighting over the issue"

In 1895, Robert Wallace MP said:

"The actual Government of this country is properly neither a Monarchy nor a Democracy, but mainly an alternation of two traditional Oligarchies...managing the members of its Parliamentary following through a dexterous blending of menace, cajolery and reward."

The wife of a senior Conservative politician has more recently described the system as being *"two party oligarchies propping each other up"*.

Peter Oborne has stated:

"Though the public is always told that Tory and Labour are in opposition, that is not really the case. They are led to believe that the Liberal Democrats are an insurgent third party, but that is not the case either. It has come to seem to me that their strongest loyalties are to each other. For the greatest part of my time as a political reporter the most bitter rivalries at Westminster have involved factional conflicts within individual parties rather than collisions of ideology and belief."

9. The Operation of an Independent Legislature

These issues with parliament are further highlighted by comparing them with other assemblies. The City of London Corporation forms the oldest government in the UK and one of the oldest local governments in the world with over one thousand years of municipal autonomy. Its proceedings have been called the "Grandmother of Parliaments".

Its Court of Common Council continues to operate its proceedings without any political parties. Each representative is elected on the basis of the preferences of the electorate and is then free, without any party pressure or whipping, to act and vote in line with his or her best judgment. Membership of committees can be decided by votes of all members. Individual members are as free to put forward their own questions and resolutions as are the City administration. No Councilman or Alderman receives any salary for their contribution.

It is sometimes said that party or collective responsibility is necessary for decisions to be made. However, as with the City of London, places like the Isle of Man operate very effectively with a majority of Independent MPs and no preponderant political parties. Similarly some councils such as Shetland and Orkney are entirely composed of Independent councillors and many councils now operate with no overall control.

In other countries, such as the US, the whipping system is much weaker, as the whips cannot bargain with a congressman by denying promotion or through other sanctions. The legislatures nevertheless operate effectively.

The only real challenge to the UK Government is now through the crossbenchers in the House of Lords who are individuals acting on the basis that they have a free vote which is not whipped by any party. The success of the Lords' crossbenchers in enforcing better discussion of Government proposals in recent years provides very strong support in favour of allowing similar discussions and votes, unfettered by party whipping, to take place in the House of Commons. It should also be noted that the crossbenchers act as a formal group, even electing their own chair, but these structures confine themselves to administrative matters and do not direct any political policy, exactly as envisaged for the Jury Team.

Writing in The Times in January 2009, Vernon Bogdanor, Professor of Government at Oxford University, said:

"In the Commons, a government can generally rely on the whips. In the Lords, it has to win the argument."

There are also specific successful examples of when MPs have been allowed to campaign separately from their party. In the 1975 referendum on continuing membership of the EEC, Government ministers were allowed to campaign as they wished. Similarly there have been free votes on issues such as abortion or fertilisation, as described above, and on others such as Sunday trading or foxhunting (although in the latter case the strong views of many Labour MPs were already well known and a whip would have added little).

The absence of the party whip does not bring chaos and in contrast leads to perfectly acceptable Parliamentary decisions which indeed usually have more credibility because it is known that MPs have exercised their own judgment rather than just being lobby fodder.

10. The Wisdom of Crowds

The philosophy of the wisdom of crowds, well described in James Surowiecki's 2004 book, endorses the concepts of the Jury Team especially by demonstrating how larger groups of independently acting individuals are likely to make decisions better than either individuals or small groups. Surowiecki shows that the three elements required to get the best decisions are that the large group should have:

- Diversity of Opinion
  Each person should have private information even if it is just their own interpretation of the known facts.

- Independence
  People's opinions should be individual and not determined by the opinions of those around them.

- Decentralisation
  People should be able to use their own specialisation and local knowledge.

These three factors form a key basis of the philosophy of the Jury Team. In contrast, the current party political system in Parliament negates any "Diversity of Opinion" or "Independence" and fights any "Decentralisation". It is the exact opposite of what is required to make the best decisions.

The Jury Team will therefore consist of high-quality individuals, selected by the electorate directly rather than through the existing political parties. They will be dedicated to the needs of the electors and free to use their own judgment. There is no doubt that this is more consistent with the principles of democracy.

In this way a wide group of independent people will be able to review all Government proposals and only vote for them if they believe them to be sensible. The Jury Team candidates will therefore have as the first of the Jury Team Governance Proposals:

> MPs should be free to vote in line with their best judgment and not be required to obey any party whips.

B. Making MPs Accept Normal Standards and Remuneration

1. The Background of MPs

People believe in democracy and expect their elected representatives to demonstrate its ideals. Unfortunately politicians are not now generally seen as sufficiently experienced or competent for the offices which they hold, as operating in a trustworthy manner or as being in the job for the benefit of their constituents rather than for themselves. Voters feel let down by pronouncements which turn out to be spin, by a quest for publicity rather than for real change, by pledges which are not kept and by personal issues such as corruption and seemingly extravagant expenses. Many of these issues result from the generally little proper prior career experience which MPs have had before entering the House of Commons.

Joan Bakewell wrote in The Times in January 2009:

The End Of The Party

"But it is the Commons that cries out for change. The electoral process is now so honed to serve the interests of political careers that MPs are growing more and more like each other. Learning the trade in university debating clubs, a year or two in a think-tank, then as political advisers, or rising through the grinding ranks of local councils, the political careerist is a clear type: focused and ambitious, fluent in the jargon of procedure and points of order, glib with amendments and early day motions."

The current system of political parties does not allow MPs much opportunity to make known their individual judgments and one consequence of this reduction in the role of an MP is that the job now attracts less prestigious candidates. Historically many people decided to become an MP after a successful first career as a way of involving themselves in the life of the country and of giving back some of their experience. Nowadays such people tend to choose to move into the charity world or into retirement.

In contrast, most of those now seeking to become MPs, and most of the front benches of the three main political parties, are people who have only been in the "Westminster Village" since leaving college, working as research analysts, marketing advisers, journalists or in other similar capacities.

"A political party is now a sort of glorified employment bureau for political careerists"
Jan Marijnissen

In writing in The Times about the likely attitude of many Labour MPs to what he described as "Gordon Brown's flailing leadership", Matthew Parris, a former MP, described how most MPs are more concerned with their own likely employment prospects than they are with their party's electoral prospects:

"For the great majority of the Parliamentary Labour Party with no job in government, you can largely discount the issue of Labour losing power. So long as they retain their seats they keep the job they have - that of a backbencher. You may be sure that the most pressing thing on the minds of most Labour MPs this weekend is their own majority at the next election, not their party's.

Even those MPs who have previously worked outside the immediate Westminster Village have tended to choose areas such as public relations rather than actually leading or managing in a charitable, commercial or public organisation. As a result such people tend to see the world mainly through the lens of short term media acceptance rather than longer term strategies and implementation.

People who would find it difficult to get a responsible job running the whole or part of any other significant organisation are suddenly given legitimacy by being selected by a political party and becoming MPs. A fair proportion of these, typically at least 40%, will subsequently become ministers. It is clear that there would be no likelihood of most of these people gaining an equivalent position in any other walk of life and it is therefore the endorsement of the political party label which gives them the opportunity for their apparent success in gaining a ministerial appointment.

An April 2008 study by the charity The Industry and Parliament Trust and the market research agency ComRes showed that only 21% of MPs had five or more years' experience in business management or financial services. The survey concluded: *"There is significant room for improvement in the general business-friendliness of our legislatures"* and noted that 80% of the British workforce is employed in the private sector which meant that Parliament had become seriously unrepresentative on this factor.

A January 2009 letter to The Times from J. Anderson of London said:

> *"We have, through our own apathy, allowed our government institutions to become increasingly corrupted by a cosy club of self-centered professionals who are more disconnected than ever from the real lives that most of us want to live.*
>
> *If Britain wants real leadership in government, by honest and independent-minded individuals, who put the interests of their local constituents and their country above their own and those of their party, then voters need to take collective action at the next election to remove this cross-party crop of political cronies. We need to find a new way forward.*
>
> *Overly powerful political parties, together with the professional "yes men" they select (to represent them not us), continue to*

destroy the integrity of our government institutions, to abuse our trust – and to erode the fabric of our society. We only have ourselves to blame."

2. The Behaviour of MPs

The legitimacy of Parliament depends on the trust which the public has in individual MPs and in the way in which all MPs conduct their personal and political lives. Trust is *'a bet on the future contingent action of others'*.

This trust can be damaged by the attitude of MPs at constituency level. In The Times in July 2008, Will Pavia described a letter written by David Clelland MP to one of his constituents telling him to *"stick"* his vote:

"Mr Clelland, who has represented the people of Tyne Bridge in Newcastle for 23 years, has written to one resident informing him that he had no desire for his vote in the future. "I accept your offer not to vote for me again," he wrote, in bold defiance of the usual conventions that exist in communications between elected representatives and their electorate. "I do not want your vote so you can stick it wherever best pleases you."

Mr Clelland, 64, offered this advice in response to a letter from Gary Scott, 27, an IT salesman with concerns over civil liberties. Mr Scott was very disappointed with what he saw. "You vote with your party on pretty much every single issue," he wrote. "It's not your constituents you represent, it's your party."

Mr Clelland replied accusing Mr Scott of arrogance for thinking that "you . . . represent the views of the people of our community". This, Mr Clelland wrote, was his job.

Mr Clelland is the not the first Honourable Member to have allowed his true feelings to be heard. On announcing his intention to step down from Parliament, Tony Banks said that working with his constituents had been "intellectually numbing" and "tedious in the extreme".

On another occasion an aide to Dari Taylor, MP, advised his boss that there was "no rush" to help a constituent who was a "snotty" woman who "hates the Government". The advice was accidentally e-mailed directly to the constituent. Michael Stern, MP for Bristol North West until 1997, named one of his constituents as a "neighbour from hell".

Although there are many MPs who do not misuse their position, in the last forty years there have been a number of government scandals which have eroded people's trust in MPs. These include the 1972 Poulson scandal when a Select Committee decided that the then Home Secretary and two other MPs had acted improperly. In the 1990s two Conservative MPs admitted they had accepted "cash for questions", there were allegations about others accepting bribes and a number of personal scandals which led to the word "sleaze" coming into common use. More recently Peter Mandelson resigned twice from Tony Blair's Cabinet for impropriety although he was subsequently reappointed by Gordon Brown.

"All political parties die at last of swallowing their own lies"
~ John Arbuthnot

As a result of the political scandals during his Government, John Major set up the (Nolan) Committee on Standards in Public Life. The political scientist, Ivor Crewe, testified to that Committee.

"There is no doubt that distrust and alienation has risen to a higher level than ever before. It was always fairly prevalent; it is now in many regards almost universal."

Similarly Andrew Marr, the journalist, wrote in 1995:

"Most people don't feel oppressed by their politicians, merely a bit contemptuous of them".

Unfortunately the establishment of the Nolan Committee has not substantially increased public confidence. Surveys in 2004 showed only 16% of voters felt that standards in public life had improved, that only 17% of the public thought that MPs showed a "high moral code" and that only 27% trusted them generally.

The Nolan Committee's own 2008 research report states: *"There is evidence in the 2008 survey to suggest that satisfaction with standards of conduct in public office has declined since the last survey was conducted in 2006:*

- *More people rate standards of conduct of public office holders overall as 'low' in 2008 than in 2006*

- *More think that conduct has deteriorated over the past few years*

- *They are less confident that the authorities are committed to upholding standards of conduct or that public office holders will be punished for doing wrong*

- *They are less satisfied with the way in which Government ministers perform their jobs – in particular in the extent to which they keep in touch with what people think is important, tell the truth and use their power for their own gain"*

As Niall FitzGerald of Unilever put it: "*Trust can't be built in a one-off spate of advertising. It is built over the long term, on the basis not of communication but of action"*

A mood of discontent about the political system not only permeates the population in total but also exists amongst backbench MPs themselves. They wonder if their role is really a worthwhile one in the light of what they can actually achieve with the very little real power that they have while being constantly criticised over their behaviour and expenses.

3. <u>The Voting Record of MPs</u>

Many of the activities of MPs are difficult to measure objectively. However the right of MPs to vote is one of the primary purposes of their being in Parliament and therefore the voting record of MPs is of interest to the electorate and is public. In general it shows that MPs are not as assiduous in the decision lobbies as they may appear to claim.

There are a number of well known special reasons why MPs may not vote frequently. For instance the five Sinn Fein MPs refuse to take the Oath of Allegiance and are therefore unable to vote. Similarly the Party leaders tend to have low voting records. In the last session Gordon Brown attended only about 17% of the votes in the House of Commons and David Cameron only about 27%.

In the 2006-7 session there were just 221 votes. A fair measure of voting attendance might be to expect MPs to attend a minimum of 75% of the votes that take place. However a recent analysis published on the website *www.publicwhip.org.uk* (and excluding for each party those who act as Speaker or Deputy Speaker) showed that of the 193 Conservative MPs, 177 (92%) of them failed to vote at least three quarters of the time. The equivalent figures show that of the 349 Labour MPs, 119 (34%) voted on less than three-quarters of the possible occasions and of the 63 Liberal Democrat MPs, 55 (87%) failed to achieve this level.

Websites such as *www.theyworkforyou.com* give detailed information for each MP about how they voted on particular issues, the subjects on which they asked Parliamentary questions, the committees to which they belong, their declaration of interests and their expenses. The website *www.revolts.co.uk*, run by Philip Cowley, gives further information about MPs' voting behaviour.

4. <u>Parliament as a Workplace</u>

MPs have a privileged lifestyle at Westminster as Parliament is still located in what is legally a Royal Palace. Many of the normal laws of the land affecting ordinary citizens, such as drinking hours, do not therefore affect MPs' lifestyles.

The staff of the House of Commons itself averaged 1,696 during 2007-8, an increase of 12% from the 1,520 employed in 2003-4. These include around 200 in the Commons library and 300 in the catering department who provided 1,519,000 meals to MPs and their staff during 2007-8. The total cost of the House of Commons is about £200 million, around £300,000 a member in addition to their own costs (salary, pension, tax and expenses) of about £250,000, a total cost of over half a million pounds per MP per year or a total of £350 million.

During the 2007-8 session the House of Commons met for just 153 days (similar to the 146 days of 2006-7), an average of less than three days per week. The sittings lasted 1,201 hours. With the total cost of £350 million this means the expense of running the Commons was about £2.3 million per sitting day or £300,000 per sitting hour.

The End Of The Party

The 3rd December 2008 Queen's Speech to open the 2008-9 Parliamentary year has been mandated by the Government to be debated in 128 days of Parliamentary time, the shortest number of scheduled Parliamentary days since 1979. As no plans have been announced to decrease the costs of MPs or Parliamentary staff, and with salary and pension cost inflation for MPs and Parliamentary staff, this further 16% reduction in the number of sitting days means that the cost of the House of Commons will rise to more than £360,000 per sitting hour, about £100 per second or the average wage of a UK employee every four minutes.

The total costs could be cut by reducing the number of MPs. David Cameron has suggested a reduction of 60 as reported by Nicholas Watt of the Guardian in January 2009:

"David Cameron would remove more than 60 MPs as part of a Tory plan to make parliament work more efficiently. Drawing on plans drawn up by Kenneth Clarke, the former chancellor, the Tory leader today pledges to introduce legislation in his first term as prime minister to cut the size of the Commons by 10%. There are currently 646 MPs, a figure that is due to increase to 650 at the next election.

Cameron tells today's Financial Times: "I think the House of Commons could do the job that it does with 10% fewer MPs without any trouble at all."... I believe in having seats that are the same size all across the country."

Cameron would reduce the number of Welsh seats from 40 to around 30 and would cut small inner-city constituencies. These changes would benefit the Tories."

In 2005 the total UK electorate was 44,261,545 and the UK's largest constituency was the Isle of Wight with an electorate of 108,253. If all the constituencies were around the same size as the Isle of Wight then there would only need to be 409 MPs. This is closely in line with the actual 420 seating places in the House of Commons and would therefore allow each MP to have their own seat. Compared to the current 646 seats, this is a reduction of 235 MPs or 37%. This would give a cost saving in MPs' salaries and expenses of about £60 million plus additional House of Commons savings on catering and other costs of over £50 million.

5. MPs' and Ministers' Remuneration

An MP currently has an annual salary of £63,291. In addition London MPs also receive a London Weighting Allowance of £7,500 which was increased by 157% from the previous figure of £2,916 in a Commons vote on the 3rd July 2008. This was reported by the London Evening Standard:

"Thirteen government members including Harriet Harman will get an inflation-busting pay rise next year, the Evening Standard can reveal. They are among 26 London MPs whose Commons pay will increase by up to 9.4 per cent from 1 April under a deal voted through before the summer recess. The cash bonanza flies in the face of the Government's official policy of pay restraint - and will benefit ministers who have voted to hold down pay for police and nurses.

Altogether the MPs will get increases of about £6,000 each next year, made up of the annual rise that all MPs receive plus a huge one-off increase in the pay top-up that MPs with London constituencies are allowed to claim.

Olympics Minister Tessa Jowell voted for it, however, as did Justice Minister Bridget Prentice and Labour whip Siobhain McDonagh. All three support the Government's policy of holding down public sector pay to around 2.5 per cent.

The TaxPayers' Alliance condemned the rises. Spokesman Mark Wallace said: "Next time these ministers say they understand what ordinary people are going through, everyone should remember they have protected themselves from the soaring cost of living, while the rest of us foot the bill."

Ministers receive a separate salary in addition to the salary of £63,291 received by them as MPs. The additional rate for the four key levels of minister is:

	£
Prime Minister	128,174
Cabinet Minister	76,904
Minister of State	39,893
Parliamentary Under Secretary of State	30,280

However ministers have to be fully committed to their official duties and therefore have less time for their constituencies. They are also of course prohibited from actively scrutinising or criticising Government policy in Parliament. This used to be recognised by the Top Salaries Review Body with ministers only receiving two thirds of the MPs salary in addition to their ministerial salary. This practice has however been discontinued and ministers now receive both full salaries.

A similar anomaly relates to MPs from Scotland, Wales and Northern Ireland who have less of a constituency workload because many of the areas of most interest to their constituents such as health and education are no longer the responsibility in those nations of the Westminster Parliament and are dealt with by their local representatives.

In addition to the 646 Westminster MPs there are now 129 MSPs in Scotland, 108 MLAs in Northern Ireland and 60 AM/ACs in Wales and these 287 people and their staffs take on a lot of the constituency workload previously undertaken from Westminster. In a Commons debate in July 2007, former Conservative Party leader Michael Howard said *"Devolution in Wales and Scotland has already created two classes of MPs"*. The then Liberal Democrat leader Sir Menzies Campbell said reform was *"long overdue"* and he called for a *"constitutional convention"* to discuss changes.

These anomalies all need to be reviewed independently so that there is a proper salary structure for backbench English MPs, for MPs who are from one of the devolved nations, and for MPs who are also ministers, with an agreed relationship between their respective remuneration packages.

6. MPs' Expenses and Allowances

"Faction seldom leaves a man honest, however it might find him"
~ Samuel Johnson

The issue of expenses is a particularly sensitive one for many voters. It has become clear that MPs have become used to using taxpayers money, even within the rules, in a way which would never be sanctioned in any other charitable, commercial or public organisation. This includes housing expenses when other housing is available, relatively excessive personal purchases (the John

Lewis list) and the employment of relatives without any proper independent selection procedure or appraisal.

Examples of fiddling expenses outside the rules include one Conservative MP who wrongly claimed over £90,000 in housing allowances. Another was involved with a firm which offered paid tours and dinners at the Palace of Westminster in clear breach of the rules. However in both cases the MPs concerned just announced their retirement and were not fined or subject to any criminal sanctions

In addition to their £63,291 salary, Members can claim the following annual allowances:

	£
Staffing Allowance	100,205
Pension Provision for Members' staff	10,020
Additional Costs Allowance	24,006
Incidental Expenses Allowance	22,193
Communications Allowance	10,400
IT equipment	5,000
Total	171,824

The House of Commons Library provides the following further information about MPs' traveling, termination and pension expenses:

- Members are currently provided with corporate travel cards that may be used to purchase travel tickets, for journeys by rail, sea or air on Parliamentary business. These cover journeys within the triangle of home, constituency and Westminster. Members may also use parking spaces, for which no charge is made, in the Parliamentary car park. Journeys may also be made by the spouse, and children under the age of 18, of a Member between London and the constituency and/or London and home by rail, air or sea. In addition MPs have a car mileage allowance of 40p per mile for the first 10,000 miles and 25p thereafter, a motorcycle allowance of 24p per mile and a bicycle allowance of 20p per mile, all available in the same triangle as the other travel allowances. Costs of journeys outside this triangle, on Parliamentary business, may also be reimbursed if the Member notifies the Operations Directorate at least three days in advance – the three day rule may be waived in exceptional circumstances.

- Members are also reimbursed for the cost of traveling on Parliamentary duties between the United Kingdom and any European Union institution in Brussels, Luxembourg or Strasbourg or the national Parliament of a member of the Council of Europe or the European Union or of any candidate member of the EU. The scheme allows the aggregate of the cost of a return business class airfare from a London airport to one of the designated destinations and twice the corresponding civil service class A standard subsistence rate in operation.

- A "Resettlement Grant" is paid to assist with the costs of adjusting to "non-Parliamentary life" to any person who ceases to be an MP at a General Election, based on age and length of service, and varies between 50% and 100% of the annual salary payable to an MP at the time of the Dissolution.

- A "Winding-Up Allowance and Resettlement Grant" of up to one third of the annual Staffing Allowance and Incidental Expenses Allowance is paid for the reimbursement of the cost of any work on Parliamentary business undertaken on behalf of a defeated or retiring Member after the date of cessation of Membership.

- MPs get a pension accruing at 1/40th for every year of service (so after 20 years, for instance, they get half their salary as an inflation-proofed pension) for which they pay 10% of salary and the Government pays 26.8%. This compares with a 1/60th civil service scheme.

In July 2008, the House of Commons voted against proposals to limit and regularise their expense claims, as reported by Sam Coates of The Times:

"Parliament's reputation took another battering yesterday when MPs threw out plans to overhaul their expenses, insisting on their right to buy kitchens, televisions and sofas on the taxpayer. Plans for rigorous external audits, a reduction of the threshold of receipts from £25 to zero and a ban on furniture or home

improvements were all thrown out by MPs who voted against the plan by a majority of 28.

The £24,000 allowance for maintaining a second home will now remain in place and the major elements of a six-month review, set up after the Tory MP Derek Conway was found to be wrongly paying his son, will be ditched. MPs will now only be subject to internal checks, while more generous proposals for MPs' offices were approved.

Nick Harvey, the Liberal Democrat who drew up the reforms, said: "An opportunity to put our house in order and be seen to put our house in order has been passed up. They took all the nice bits but not the ones they didn't like. They took the spoonful of sugar but refused the medicine."

Sir Christopher Kelly, the chairman of the independent Committee for Standards in Public Life, said that the vote could cause *"even greater distrust of the political class"*.

As well as the reforms being defeated by 172 to 144, 325 MPs, including the Prime Minister, did not vote at all. An analysis of the vote shows that the abstentions were spread across all of the parties:

	Against Reform	For Reform	Tellers /Sp.	Abstain	Total	% Abstain
Lab	149	52	2	147	350	42.0%
Cons	20	54	1	118	193	61.1%
LDem	0	35	1	27	63	42.9%
Other	3	3	1	33	40	82.5%
Total	172	144	5	325	646	50.3%

The number of abstentions in either of the two major parties would have been enough easily to overturn the majority vote against reforms.

In January 2009, Harriet Harman announced that despite the long-running campaign to put MPs on the same basis as other public officials in providing details of their expenses, a special

Statutory Instrument would be enacted to allow MPs to hide this information. This was reported by David Hencke of The Guardian as follows:

"Ministers are poised to exempt all MPs and peers from having to publish details of their expenses, only weeks before MPs were due to be forced to disclose more than 1.2 million receipts covering claims for the last three years.

The move next week will allow parliament to nullify all the long-fought victories by campaigners and journalists to force MPs to publish details of all their individual receipts for their second homes, including details of what they spent on furnishings, maintenance, rent, mortgage payments, staffing, travel, office staffing and equipment.

The changes will be retrospective and all pending requests for more information under the Freedom of Information Act will be blocked. The changes will put MPs and peers in a special category as the only paid public officials who will not have to disclose the full details of their expenses and allowances. In Scotland, MSPs are required to declare all of their expenses to the Scottish parliament.

Harriet Harman, leader of the house, is understood to have pressed for the change after being lobbied by the Conservative 1922 backbench committee and the parliamentary Labour party committee, which both wanted to stop the release of the information

Matthew Elliott of the TaxPayers' Alliance said: 'It is an absolute disgrace that the government is going to such absurd lengths to keep MPs' expenses secret from the very people who pay the bills. These desperate measures will only harm parliament's standing by making people wonder what it is that politicians have to hide.' "

The Guardian commented in an Editorial:

"Parliamentarians are obviously entitled to privacy. They are also right to worry that some requests aim to tarnish the reputation of

all politicians. But for MPs to seek to hide from rules that they have imposed on every other public body is a mistake

Rewriting the law to keep the money but limit scrutiny is no way to win back trust."

However, as reported by Jon Ungoed-Thomas in The Sunday Times, the government eventually backed down as a result of public lobbying over the Internet:

"When the television correspondent Martin Bell became an independent MP, he was astonished to discover the laxity of the expenses system. He said he was invited to "sign a cheque to myself every month right up to the limit". The High Court ruled in a case last year that details of claims by 14 MPs should be disclosed. The High Court ruling implied that details of all MPs' expenses claims would have to be made public. So the government decided on its plan to exempt the records from freedom of information laws. It underestimated the backlash. Unlock Democracy, the campaign group, took an advertisement in The Times describing the move as "shameless". Thousands of people signed online petitions and MPs were bombarded with letters and e-mails condemning the move.

Details of all MPs' expenses claims between 2004 and 2008 should now be published (with certain personal information removed). From the claims of the 14 MPs whose expenses have already been released, it emerged that Margaret Beckett, now housing minister, used public funds to help with gardening bills at her home and Barbara Follett a Labour minister married to Ken Follett, the millionaire author, paid for window cleaners."

In February 2009 Ben Russell reported in The Independent that Jacqui Smith, the Home Secretary, was under investigation:

"The Home Secretary, Jacqui Smith, is being investigated by the parliamentary sleaze watchdog over her expenses claims for a second home.

John Lyon, the parliamentary commissioner for standards, asked Ms Smith for a formal response to allegations from her neighbours that she often spends just two nights a week at the London address she classes as her main home. Ms Smith's declaration that her primary residence is her sister's house in south-east London, where she pays £100 a week rent for a room, has allowed her to claim £116,000 in second-home allowance over five years for her family home in Redditch, Worcestershire, where her husband and children live."

An Editorial in The Daily Telegraph in February 2009 was entitled *Humbug of politicians with their allowances* and said:

"It is rare for a week to go by nowadays without fresh evidence emerging of politicians milking their generous, self-regulated, systems of allowances and expenses for all they are worth. Jacqui Smith, the Home Secretary, continues to insist she "abided by the rules" when designating her sister's home in south London where she lodges as her main residence, thus enabling her to claim up to £24,000 a year in housing allowance. Michael Ancram, the former Conservative chairman, says that he only claims "what I have always been told I am entitled to claim" after eyebrows were raised over a £20,000 payment that included, among other things, the cost of clearing moss from his garden.

Here we have one of the few areas of genuine cross-party consensus at Westminster. MPs of every stripe cleave to the idea that their allowances are there to be claimed, regardless – it seems – of whether they cover genuine outgoings. These are the same people who have led the protests against bankers' bonuses, failing to see the humbug in this when they themselves table hefty, six-figure expenses claims each year that are subjected to only the most perfunctory of checks because, as honourable men and women, MPs are expected to maintain the highest standards of probity.

There is a common thread running through all this and that is the desuetude of the notion of public service. The time when a man or woman would make their mark in one walk of life before going into politics to use the experience so gathered to "put something back" is long gone. Unfortunately, when politics is treated as just a career, not a calling, it is inevitable that many of its practitioners will slip into the habit of chiselling what they can out of it. Gordon Brown yesterday called for a return to "traditional" banking values where bankers are the "servants not the masters". Substitute the word political for banking and MPs for bankers and that is a sentiment we would all enthusiastically endorse."

It is essential that MPs are seen as operating under the same constraints as apply to their electorate in terms of their salaries and expenses, especially as public money is involved. The civil service has a clear policy on salaries and expenses.

The Jury Team Governance Proposals therefore include that all MPs should be subject to the same regime as senior civil servants.

An independent commission would be established to decide which grade of civil servant is currently equivalent to an MP and salaries and expenses would then be increased for MPs in line with the average for all employees in the country (not in line with civil service pay as MPs have direct control of this).

> MPs, ministers and their political staff should be paid according to civil service pay scales, should have any expenses approved only in line with established civil service guidelines and must act according to the Nolan Principles that apply to all public bodies.

C. Policing the Politicians

1. The Current Incestuous Complaints System

As a result of public concern with certain activities of the police force, the Independent Police Complaints Commission was set up. This investigates specific defined events, such as when a member of the public is killed by a policeman on duty, and can also respond to complaints from the general public. It is properly independent and has helped to investigate and determine the validity of various actions by the police.

Unfortunately the politicians have not seen fit to set up an equivalent body to investigate their own behaviour:

- Any sanctions against MPs or Lords for their activities are decided by other MPs or Lords who may well have, or at least be seen to have, a vested interest in maintaining generous arrangements and flexibility for their colleagues.

- Similarly the appointment and resignation of ministers is solely in the hands of the Prime Minister who is inevitably biased towards protecting the reputation of the minister concerned in order to try to prevent this from rebounding on the reputation of his or her party

2. MPs' and Lords' Conduct

Following the various scandals about MPs, there is now a Parliamentary Commissioner for Standards. However in relation to any accusations of misconduct this role only involves being a collector of evidence which is then presented to the House of Commons Privileges Committee. (Previous holders of the office have indicated that they have often had a difficult time in getting evidence from MPs.) It is then the Committee which decides on any sanctions although it wields limited powers in practice which normally relate just to the suspension of the MP for a matter of days.

The position in the House of Lords on sanctions for wrongful behaviour is even less clear as Lords hold their titles for life.

Following the revelations about certain Lords being alleged to have been prepared to accept cash in return for influencing legislation, Sam Coates wrote in The Times in January 2009:

"The House of Lords faces fresh "cash for amendments" accusations today after The Times discovered that a Labour peer proposed changes in the law that would benefit companies he was paid to represent.

Lord O'Neill of Clackmannan put down amendments this month to the Construction Bill that would have given commercial advantage to building subcontractors by allowing them greater legal protection when claiming payments.

The peer, who until 2005 was a long-serving MP, withdrew the amendments 48 hours ago. He felt it "inappropriate in the current climate to pursue them" after corruption allegations surfaced against four peers at the weekend, his spokesman said.

The House of Lords insists that such behaviour is entirely within the rules – because he is not accepting money in return for pursuing a specific change to the law. The existence of this loophole, however, will add weight to the critics who say that the outside interests of peers are having a corrosive effect on the Upper House."

Similarly in a report entitled "Most of Tory team in Lords have second jobs" Jean Eaglesham, Chief Political Correspondent, stated in the Financial Times in January 2009:

"Two-thirds of David Cameron's front-bench team in the Lords have paid outside jobs, some of which present a potential conflict of interest with the peers' official parliamentary roles, analysis by the FT has revealed. Labour attacked the Tories' slew of second jobs on Friday as the escalating row over peers' outside interests increased pressure for reform of the second chamber. Ministers are banned from having paid outside jobs but no such bar applies to their Tory shadows. No fewer than 18 out of the 27 peers on the Conservative front bench have paid directorships, consultancies or other outside employment. Several potential conflicts of interests could arise from the second jobs held by the shadow ministers".

In other areas of public service, and indeed in the private sector, any employee found guilty of corruption or fiddling expenses is likely to be heavily disciplined and probably reported to the police. It is quite clear that the criminal law applies to all such incidents outside Parliament and there is no reason why it should not also do so for MPs and Lords. It is vital if respect for Parliament is to be increased that the public has faith that MPs and Lords are subject to the same sanctions as themselves if they go against the agreed rules and either misspend public money or act in an improper way.

This was described in a letter to The Times in January 2009:

"Sir, It is sad that so few people in public life seem to have any idea as to basic right or wrong. That lobbying and financial reward is even considered is bad enough; legislators must be savvy enough to recognise that they must be both seen to be and actually be impartial.

But then when problems and incidents occur, as they will do from time to time, not only do the individuals concerned cling to office with the flimsiest of excuses, but colleagues and officials appear to collude and assist by placing the most generous of interpretations on others' actions; that is if they can muster the energy to investigate in the first place.

The alleged actions of the lords as reported, if mirrored in ordinary business life, would be considered as corruption and treated as such. Is it too much to ask that our lawmakers abide by the same laws and standards as apply to the rest of us?

Nick Tyler, Sanderstead, Surrey"

3. Ministerial Conduct

Ministers are subject to The Ministerial Code of Conduct which is set out in a booklet that is required reading of all ministers. However any ministers who violate the Code are only subject to whatever investigation the Prime Minister feels is suitable. Typically the Prime Minister, who is the sole judge and jury of any breaches, will try to defend his or her ministers for as long as possible, often leading to further damaging revelations becoming public.

Occasionally ministerial resignations will be accepted by a Prime Minister in order to end speculation about a particular policy but the minister may well be reappointed to a different position as happened in 1967 when James Callaghan resigned as Chancellor of the Exchequer but was immediately appointed as Home Secretary.

Prime Ministers can delay any reckoning by setting up enquiries such as with Lord Justice Scott in relation to the Arms to Iraq scandal. Even though the Scott enquiry explicitly stated that three ministers had provided *"inaccurate and misleading*" answers to Parliament, the then prime minister, John Major, continued to resist calls for any ministerial resignation.

Lord Hutton held an enquiry into the case of Dr David Kelly who committed suicide in relation to reports of "sexing up" the Iraq Dossier. Ipsos/MORI commented on the Hutton Report:

"The public's lack of faith in politicians is highlighted in reaction to the Hutton Report on the circumstances leading to the death of Dr

Kelly. The eminence of the judge did not stop 48% still believing that the Prime Minister lied about his role in Dr Kelly's exposure (according to ICM for The Guardian) and 56% believing that 'Lord Hutton as a member of the establishment was too ready to sympathise with the Government' (YouGov for The Telegraph)."

There are many instances of ministers not resigning when the public would have expected a resignation or sacking in similar circumstances in any other organisation. A list of these was provided by Michael Rush in his book *Parliament Today*. These include a varied series of errors such as the misleading of prospective pensioners about changes to SERPS, the BSE outbreak, the Millennium Dome, arms to Sierra Leone and Passport Agency delays.

The Prime Minister now has an independent adviser to ascertain the facts when the Ministerial Code may have been breached. The first holder of this post was Sir John Bourn, appointed in 2006, but he was not asked to carry out any investigations of ministers although he did make a number of investigations and reports on the returns that ministers had made under Section 5 (Ministers and Civil Servants) of the Ministerial Code. In accordance with the terms of his appointment, his advice was private and confidential. The current incumbent is Sir Philip Mawer.

The Government is still resisting any move to allow the independent adviser to decide what to investigate or to be able to report publicly. This was confirmed in the Government's response to the Ninth Special Report of the Commons Public Administration Committee, October 2008, which included these paragraphs:

> Committee: *For the avoidance of doubt, therefore, we invite the Prime Minister to state unambiguously that he will make public any relevant findings of fact.*
>
> Government response: *The Government believes that it is important for the Prime Minister to be able to make decisions after a balanced consideration of the facts of an individual case. It must therefore be for the Prime Minister to account for his decision, including making public any findings of relevant fact.*

> Committee: *It is hard to see how the Independent Adviser can command public confidence if the Prime Minister can decide that prima facie breaches of the Code will not be investigated.*
>
> Government response: *In deciding whether or not to refer a matter to the independent adviser for investigation, the Prime Minister will wish to take into account a range of factors, including whether the facts are already known. In line with the Government's response to the Committee's recommendation 5, the Government believes it must ultimately be for the Prime Minister to account to Parliament for his decisions and actions in relation to the appointment of his Ministers.*

Prime Ministers defend their ministerial colleagues because it otherwise could be bad for their party. One of the additional advantages of the Jury Team proposals is that it would be easier for the Prime Minister to fire a minister as there would be no party to defend. In the fullness of time the appointment and firing of ministers could become a matter for the relevant Select Committee.

It is clearly unacceptable for MPs, Lords or Ministers not to be subject to proper independent investigation and, if necessary, sanction if they have violated the agreed rules. It has become quite clear that self policing either by the Privileges Committee or by the Prime Minister is not only ineffective but undermines public confidence. The Jury Team therefore proposes the setting up of an independent Politicians Complaints Commission modeled on the Independent Police Complaints Commission.

4. The Principles that should Apply

The seven 'Nolan' Principles of Public Life are now well established in all parts of the public sector. They should clearly also apply to MPs, Lords and ministers and should be the basis of the principles used by the independent Politicians Complaints Commission to decide on issues which come before it

> Selflessness
> Holders of public office should take decisions solely in terms of the public interest. They should not do so in order

to gain financial or other material benefits for themselves, their family, or their friends.

Integrity
Holders of public office should not place themselves under any financial or other obligation to outside individuals or organisations that might influence them in the performance of their official duties.

Objectivity
In carrying out public business, including making public appointments, awarding contracts, or recommending individuals for awards or benefits, holders of public office should make choices on merit.

Accountability
Holders of public office are accountable for their decisions and actions to the public and must submit themselves to whatever scrutiny is appropriate to their office.

Openness
Holders of public office should be as open as possible about all the decisions and actions they take. They should give reasons for their decisions and restrict information only when the wider public interest clearly demands.

Honesty
Holders of public office have a duty to declare any private interests relating to their public duties and to take steps to resolve any conflicts arising in a way that protects the public interest.

Leadership
Holders of public office should promote and support these principles by leadership and example.

5. Appointments to Government Bodies

The appointment of members of independent commissions is itself fraught with political difficulty under current arrangements. During the 1990s ministers were criticised for appointing their political cronies to quangos and other Government jobs. As a result the process has moved on but now it is largely senior civil servants who control and sit on appointment panels for most Government jobs. This is so even for quangos designed to give independent, and if necessary contrary, advice to the Government. This is in itself unacceptable as it is inappropriate that a permanent secretary or other senior official should be involved in choosing the members of a quango whose statutory role may well be to critique the department concerned or to act as an umpire between Government and private individuals or organisations.

This issue was recognised in the establishment of the Judicial Appointments Commission which is designed to recommend lawyers to become judges. In order to reduce any political interference it was finally agreed by the Government that the members of the Judicial Appointments Commission would be agreed through panels themselves chosen by bodies other than the Government.

This same principle needs to be applied to the membership of the independent Politicians Complaints Commission which would probably have nine members, each appointed for a term of three years (with staggered initial arrangements) and a maximum tenure of nine years. The nine positions would be widely advertised. A set of seven NGOs (non-governmental organisations) would be designated by the Office of the Commissioner for Public Appointments and agreed by Parliament and would each nominate a member of an appointments panel with responsibility for appointing the members of the Commission. Suitable NGOs in this case might be the Institute of Business Ethics, Police Federation, Magistrates Association, Confederation of British Industry, Trades Union Congress, National Council for Voluntary Organisations and the Chartered Management Institute (one of these organisations, chosen by ballot in the first six years, would step down each year and a new one appointed so as to prevent any ossification).

An independent Politicians Complaints Commission, modeled on the Independent Police Complaints Commission, with its Board appointed by a panel of designated NGOs, should be established to investigate accusations about national and local politicians, basing its judgments on the Nolan principles that apply to all public bodies.

D. Legitimising the Funding of Political Parties

1. The Lack of General Financial Support

The problems of funding political parties are a symptom of the problems which parties have in modern society. The great majority of people do not want to give money to a political party. They may support it at an election but they are not even prepared to give it annually the cash equivalent of the cost of a DVD (for instance the Conservative Party annual subscription is normally £15). If political parties cannot get money from a wide proportion of the population then they are forced to go to specific funders.

Party political funding is a major concern of voters. There is a huge suspicion that those donating large sums are able to influence party policies. This thesis has credibility given the concentration of power in the party oligarchies with few checks or balances. The lack of any independence among MPs and any proper independent scrutiny by either Select Committees or Departments leads to the suspicion that party leaders can have their view of an issue changed by a donor and that it will then become law.

2. High Value Donations

Examples have included the affair of Bernie Ecclestone, head of Formula 1, where it has emerged that he and Max Mosley met Tony Blair on the 16th October 1997. Ecclestone and Mosley were both Labour Party donors and argued for a proposed ban on cigarette advertising on racing cars to be lifted. On the 17th November Blair apologised for his Government's mishandling of the affair and stated "the decision to exempt Formula One from tobacco sponsorship was taken two weeks later." However it is now clear that Blair instructed his staff to change the tobacco ban within a few hours, and not two weeks, of the meeting.

In March 2006, it was reported that the House of Lords Appointments Commission had blocked three Labour Party nominations for peerages (Dr Chai Patel, Barry Townsley and Sir David Garrard) and were investigating Robert Edmiston, a Conservative Party donor and chairman of the Midlands Industrial Council, who was also nominated for a peerage.

Following these revelations, the Labour Party disclosed the names of 12 businessmen who had given commercial loans to the party:

- Sir David Garrard – £2.3m - Property Developer
- Lord Sainsbury of Turville – £2m
- Richard Caring - £2m – International Clothing Designs
- Dr Chai Patel - £1.5m – Founder of the Priory Clinic
- Andrew Rosenfeld - £1m – Chairman of Minerva
- Rod Aldridge - £1m – Executive Chairman of Capita
- Professor Sir Christopher Evans - £1m – Biotechnology
- Barry Townsley - £1m – Stockbroker.
- Gordon Crawford - £500K – Software entrepreneur
- Derek Tullet - £400K – Financier; CBE 1997
- Sir Gulam Noon - £220K – Food empire
- Nigel Morris - £50K – Capital One, US credit card company

A week later the Conservative Party published a list of 13 benefactors who were currently loaning them a total of £16m:

- Lord Laidlaw – donations £2.7m, loans £3.5m
- Lord Ashcroft – donations £938K, loans £3.6m
- Jonas Eliasch – loans £2.6m – Boss of Head NV
- Michael Hintze - £2.5m – Hedge funds
- Henri Angest – donations £636K, loans £550K
- Lady Victoria de Rothschild – donations £129K, loans £1m
- Raymond Richards (deceased) – loans £1m
- Nigel Alliance – donations £56K, loans £450K – N Brown
- Lord Steinberg – loans £250K – Stanley Leisure
- Dame Vivien Duffield – loans £250K
- Charles Wigoder – donations £20K, loans £100K – CEO of Telecom Plus
- Alan Lewis – loans £100K – Former Conservative treasurer
- Graham Facks-Martin – loans £50K – Retired farmer

An example of the possible influencing of policy by donors was given in an article in The Times by Sam Coates in February 2009 which was entitled *Union threatens to cut its aid to Labour over Royal Mail row*:

"The Labour Party will lose the support of the postal workers' union in the forthcoming European elections if it fails to back down over the part-privatisation of the Royal Mail. Gordon Brown, who is already preparing for defeat in the European poll, is almost certain to lose the support of the Communication Workers' Union (CWU), one of the most effective campaigning groups.

The CWU, which is leading the battle against the part-privatisation, would provide a lump sum of cash in May and help on the ground in the weeks running up to polling day. A spokesman for the CWU said this help would be withdrawn if the Bill was still going through Parliament, and would act as the first step to disaffiliation from the Labour Party if it became law. The group donates about £1 million a year to the Labour Party."

3. <u>Investigations into Donations</u>

Tony Blair was involved in the "Loans for Lords/Cash for Peerages" police investigation about the alleged offering of peerages in return for interest free loans to the Labour Party. In April 2006 Des Smith, an adviser to Downing Street, was arrested in connection with police investigations but later released on bail. In July Lord Levy, the Labour Party's chief fundraiser, was arrested and questioned and two Government ministers, Lord Sainsbury of Turville and Ian McCartney, were also questioned by police. In October Michael Howard, the former leader of the Conservative Party, was also interviewed by police and in December Tony Blair was interviewed by police at 10 Downing Street and John McTernan, the Prime Minister's political secretary, was interviewed under caution by the police about a Downing Street email trail.

In January 2007, Ruth Turner, the director of Government relations at Downing Street, was arrested under caution and bailed without charge after questioning, Jack McConnell, Scotland's First Minister, was questioned as a witness by police about his nomination of Colin Boyd, Tony Blair was interviewed for a second time as a witness and Lord Levy was arrested for a second time on suspicion of honours offences and conspiracy to pervert the course of justice. In March 2007 Ruth Turner alleged in writing that Lord Levy had asked her to lie for him. In June 2007 it was revealed that Tony Blair was interviewed by police for a third time. In July 2007 the Crown Prosecution Service announced that no one would face charges in the cash for honours inquiry.

In November 2007 it surfaced that Labour had received £650,000 from businessman David Abrahams who used "friends and colleagues" to donate the money to protect his privacy. The Electoral Commission announced a formal investigation and the Labour General Secretary Peter Watt resigned. It also emerged that the Deputy Leader of the Labour Party and Leader of the House, Harriet Harman, accepted a £5,000 donation from Janet Kidd, one of the people used by David Abrahams to make donations on his behalf.

The Prime Minister, Gordon Brown, announced that he had not been aware of the source of the donations until the weekend and that they would be returned as unlawful. The Labour Party's claim that its system set up to fight sleaze was "*absolutely vigorous*" was however undermined when it emerged that a vetting committee created to oversee donations had not met for two years.

Welsh Secretary and Work Secretary Peter Hain resigned in January 2008 to "*clear his name*" after the Electoral Commission referred to police his late disclosure of £103,000 donations to his Labour deputy leadership race. Potential charges were subsequently dropped because although the facts were agreed the Crown Prosecution Service could not identify which individual was legally responsible for the lack of reporting and Hain absolved himself of responsibility.

In January 2009, the House of Commons Standards and Privileges Committee criticised both Peter Hain and Jack Straw for failing to register donations. However in contrast to people who fail to obey similar requirements in the charity or commercial world, the Committee applied no fine or other similar sanction:

- The Standards Committee concluded that Hein's "*failure to register donations on this scale is both serious and substantial*". Despite this Hain was just told he should issue a personal apology on the floor of the Commons. The Committee said that the pressures of work on frontbenchers may be a factor, but added that "*we cannot accept - and we are sure that none of them would suggest - that this excuses them from their obligations under the rules of the House*".

- The Standards Committee found Jack Straw, Justice Secretary, guilty of failing to register a donation made to him in 2004 and stated that this was "*a clear, albeit inadvertent, breach of the rules of the House*". Although he had been reminded on three occasions of the need to register the donation in question, the Justice Secretary failed to do so. "*Mr Straw has called this a chapter of accidents,*" said the Committee. "*Accidents generally happen as a result of negligence, and Mr Straw has clearly been negligent in this case.*" The Committee said it was "*surprised and disappointed that, of all members, Mr Straw should have broken the rules*". Despite this the Committee recommended no further action.

In Scotland, in June 2008 the Standards, Procedures and Public Appointments Committee of the Scottish Parliament recommended a day's suspension for Wendy Alexander as a result of failure to register donations to her leadership campaign in the register of MSP's interests. She announced her resignation as Labour Party leader in Scotland.

The Conservative Party has also been embroiled in similar scandals. In January 2006 it emerged that Boris Johnson had not declared donations to his campaign for Mayor of London to the Registrar of Members Interests, although they had been declared to the Electoral Commission. George Osborne, the Shadow Chancellor, admitted that he made a "*mistake*" in his dealings in Corfu on the yacht of Oleg Deripaska, the Russian billionaire, who was also visited at the same time by Peter Mandelson. The Observer commented on this in October 2008:

"After so many scandals, these reckless politicians don't get it: Peter Mandelson appears to have learnt nothing about dangerous liaisons with rich men. Neither have the Conservatives."

The End Of The Party

In February 2009 Georgia Warren and Steven Swinford reported in The Sunday Times about a probe of Lord Ashcroft's donations to the Conservatives:

"The Electoral Commission has launched a formal investigation into donations to the Conservative Party that were channelled from overseas by Lord Ashcroft, the party's deputy chairman. The Tories could be forced to give up nearly £5m of party funding if the commission finds they have breached electoral law by accepting the donations. The Commission launched preliminary investigations six months ago after The Sunday Times revealed that £4.79m has been transferred via a chain of companies from Belize, the Central American tax haven, to Bearwood Corporate Services (BCS), a British company said to be controlled by Ashcroft. BCS is the Conservatives' biggest corporate donor and has given £4.74m to the party since February 2003.

After conducting the review, the commission found there was sufficient evidence to suggest there may have been a breach of electoral rules and launched a formal investigation on January 30. Its inquiries are likely to focus on whether BCS is "carrying on business in the UK", a legal requirement for donors.

Three years ago Ashcroft described BCS as "a small merger-broking business", but according to a former director this part of the company was sold off. It is not known what business it now carries out. BCS's registered address is that of its auditor, BDO Stoy Hayward, in Ocean Village, Southampton. Last week a receptionist confirmed that BCS was a client but said nobody from the company worked there.

A spokeswoman for the Commission said: "The commission has begun a formal investigation into whether there has been any failure to comply with the Political Parties, Elections and Referendums Act 2000 in connection with a number of donations made to the Conservative Party from Bearwood Corporate Services."

Lord Hameed was nominated for membership of the House of Lords by the Liberal Democrats after sitting on the boards of companies associated with Alpha Healthcare, which had given them £400,000 in donations. The Liberal Democrats were also tainted by the £2.4 million they received from the financier Michael Brown whose company was ruled by the High Court to be fraudulent.

4. Current Funding Position

The Electoral Commission's quarterly spending report for July to September 2008 shows that the Labour Party received major (more than £5,000) donations of £7.5 million from only 77 organisations and people and the Conservatives £4 million from only 260 organisations and people. This total number of major donors of 337 is less than one in 100,000 of the electorate of 45 million people. The Liberal Democrats raised £0.6 million. Labour's debts now stand at £15,762,280, compared with £12,113,165 owed by the Tories.

The largest Labour donor in the quarter was the union Unite which gave £0.5 million of the total of £2.1 million from the unions. This was a smaller proportion of total Labour donations from the unions than previously: in the first quarter of 2008 the unions accounted for 93% of total donations. Unite, which has given £13.4 million to Labour since Gordon Brown became Prime Minister, was however also under scrutiny because it had helped to guarantee to the Labour Party auditors, Horwath Clark Whitehill, that the Party would be a going concern for the next 12 months as required by the auditors to provide a clean audit opinion. However both Labour and Unite have refused to make the terms of the agreement public. Lord Oakeshott of Seagrove Bay, the Liberal Democrat Treasury spokesman, said:

> *"If a political party can only keep going with guarantees from outside backers those guarantees should be fully and publicly disclosed as loans or donations. Even if they are operating a millimetre within the law, Labour are clearly breaching the spirit of the law."*

5. Funding Reform

Party funding reform has been considered many times from the Houghton Committee in 1976 to the Home Affairs Select Committee in 1994, the Neill Committee in 1998, the Electoral Commission report in 2005 and the Constitutional Affairs Select Committee investigations in 2006.

The 2006 Constitutional Affairs Select Committee reported:

> *"We believe that there are problems, both actual and perceived, with the current arrangements for party funding in the UK. While parties struggle with escalating costs and a reduction in the traditional financial support base, public confidence is damaged by the fear that donors may be able to buy political influence. While the PPERA 2000 introduced closer regulation and some improved transparency, it has not finally resolved problems with the system; if anything increased transparency, by revealing the extent of and dependency on donations from a few rich individuals, corporations and trade unions, has increased the negative impact on public confidence."*

As a result of the furore surrounding the "Cash for Peerages" scandal, in March 2006 Tony Blair, announced that there would be a review of the funding of political parties to be conducted by Sir Hayden Phillips, a retired civil servant. Sir Hayden produced an initial report in March 2007 "*Strengthening Democracy: Fair and Sustainable Funding of Political Parties*", and this was then discussed between the three major parties.

Resulting from public consultation on that report, in August 2007 a draft agreement was put to the Conservative, Labour and Liberal Democrat parties by the Hayden Phillips Secretariat The purpose of that document was stated to be: *"This new approach aims to restore public trust in the probity of party finances by setting a limit on the amount which any individual or organisation can donate to a political party."*

However the parties were unable to reach agreement, each trying to maximize its own interest. Consequently after three months of trying to achieve a settlement, Sir Hayden said:

> *"The proposals I put to the three main parties in late August and published in late October were the result of many months of discussions with the parties themselves and four meetings of the inter-party talks process in the summer. They also reflected the recommendations I set*

out in March this year in a report welcomed by all the parties.

Yet while cross-party agreement on my proposals proved not to be possible, my view remains that, taken as a whole, they are both fair and balanced, and represent a significant improvement on the present situation."

It is clear that political funding is a major issue both for political parties and for the electorate. The Jury Team therefore proposes that the recommendations of the Hayden Phillips Report in relation to political donations should be accepted and made law in order to help to clean up this aspect of British politics.

6. Key Recommendations of the Hayden Phillips Report

The key provision of the Hayden Phillips Report in relation to donations was that donations to political parties from any individual or organisation should be capped at £50,000 by 2012. Any amount donated over that limit would have to be returned to the donor, or forfeited to the Electoral Commission if this was not possible.

The Hayden Phillips Report also addressed the issue of trade union donations. It saw it as legitimate for unions to make donations on behalf of their members as long as those members were aware of this and had the right not to pay. The Hayden Phillips report therefore recommended that for the 3.5 million union members who currently pay into a political fund, the Affiliation Fees paid by trade unions will be treated for the purposes of the cap as individual donations of the members.

In order to ensure that members of unions are aware of how their money is being spent he suggested the following provisions:

- *The amounts paid by individuals into a union's political fund as their contribution to the union's affiliation fee, and the money paid by that union to a political party as its affiliation fee will be the same. This one-for-one link will be transparent and auditable.*

- *The following information will be provided on all union membership application forms:*

- *an explanation of what the political fund is and the union's affiliation to a political party;*
- *an explanation of how much individual members contribute to the political fund and towards the union's affiliation fee;*
- *an explanation of the trade union member's right at any time to stop contributing to the political fund and the union's affiliation fee and clear information about how they can do this; and*
- *an explanation of the fact that if a member stops contributing, their membership subscription will be reduced accordingly.*

- *Trade union members will be reminded annually of the amount they are contributing to the union's affiliation fee and of their right to opt out of contributing to the political fund, including how they may do so.*

The Hayden Phillips Report also noted that with this increased transparency and choice for trade union members the ten-year review ballot on the existence of the political fund, which trade unions currently have to conduct, would no longer be necessary and should be removed.

These provisions on donations seem eminently sensible and the three major political parties, if motivated by the national rather than partisan interest, would have accepted them. However as they failed to do so the Jury Team proposes that:

> The Hayden Phillips Report recommendations on capping donations to political parties should be accepted and enforced.

E. Scrutinising the Government

1. The Purpose of Parliament

Parliament should scrutinise Government actions and proposals, cause amendments as appropriate, and, in extremis, change the composition of the Government. John Stuart Mill said:

"Instead of the function of governing, for which it is radically unfit, the proper office of a representative assembly is to watch and control the Government to throw the light of publicity on it; to compel a full exposition and justification of all of them which anyone considers questionable; to censor them if found condemnable, and, if the men who compose the Government abuse their trust, or fulfill it in a manner which conflicts with the deliberate sense of the nation, to expel them from office, and either expressly or virtually appoint their successors."

When the Crown was separate from Parliament and appointed its own ministers then every line of their proposals was scrutinised and debated by Parliament. Now that the executive and legislative functions have for all practicality merged, there is nothing like the same scrutiny as there was in those days. The evidence shows that the Commons' guillotined debates and enfeebled committees do not cause the executive to change its stance on any major issues.

Graham Allen, the Labour MP, states in his book *The Last Prime Minister*:

"This has produced a massive rise in executive power, completely unmatched by any corresponding growth in the power of Parliamentary scrutiny. Indeed Parliament has systematically abdicated much of its power of delay and scrutiny by allowing ministers to effect more and more changes through regulation, statutory instrument or even administrative fiat, rather than introducing primary legislation"

Both of the main political parties relish Government either because that is their current status or because they hold the hope that the electorate will "soon" eject the governing party. The optimism of the Opposition is often enhanced by opinion polls showing dissatisfaction with the party in Government. As it expects soon to be in control, the Opposition has little incentive to improve the governance of the country as, given their hope of taking over, it is in their interests to keep Parliament as acquiescent as possible and to maintain the current system of little scrutiny by Parliament.

Parliamentary time is often used not to hold the Government to account but rather with its own MPs making political points for the Government. Such supposed questions as "*May I congratulate my*

Right Honourable friend on ..." are clearly sycophantic rather than designed for scrutiny. Indeed these questions are often planted by the whips with backbench MPs who wish to impress the party hierarchy, usually the majority of backbenchers who are depending on political advancement in that party for their career.

The weakness of Parliamentary scrutiny of Government is often cited by the UK media as a justification for the vigour with which they question and challenge the Government.

2. <u>The Use of Statutory Instruments</u>

Most Government decisions are implemented through secondary legislation (regulations etc) with Statutory Instruments (governed by the Statutory Instruments Act 1946) being the mechanism by which such regulations are enacted. However Parliament now has no right to amend but only to reject them. Usually a minister just has to lay such an Instrument before Parliament and if there is no vote against it within a period of typically 40 days then under the "negative procedure" it is deemed to have been passed.

Over 3,000 Statutory Instruments are now authorised each year and only a very small proportion of these are ever reviewed by Select Committees or in any other way. Essentially as soon as they have obtained enabling primary legislation to allow such regulations to be brought in, there is no real check on what is proposed by each department.

The lack of scrutiny of Parliament is massively highlighted by its failure to prevent any proposed Statutory Instruments from becoming law. Theoretically any member of either House can put down a motion that an Instrument should be annulled but even if in the Commons the motion is signed by a large number of Members or is moved by the official Opposition it is unlikely to be debated. The last time the House of Commons annulled a Statutory Instrument was 30 years ago in 1979 when it rejected the Paraffin (Maximum Retail Prices) (Revocation) Order 1979 (SI 1979/797) since which time over 70,000 Statutory Instruments have become law.

In January 2009 the Government announced its controversial decision to go ahead with a third runway at Heathrow. At Prime Minister's Question Time, Gordon Brown failed to respond directly to a straight question from John Randall MP asking whether *"any further expansion at Heathrow will be subject to a vote in this Chamber?"* There was later a strongly whipped vote.

The same week it emerged that the Government also wanted to sidestep Parliament on the introduction of new powers to fine people who have non-recyclable waste, as reported by David Leppard of The Times:

"The Government has quietly adopted powers enabling it to introduce national pay-as-you-throw rubbish taxes of up to £100 without a vote in parliament. The move, which was confirmed this weekend by the Department for Environment, Food and Rural Affairs (Defra), will allow councils across the country to impose extra charges on householders who leave out too much non-recyclable waste.

The fact that ministers have adopted powers to impose the taxes on millions of households without a vote in the Commons will shock MPs. They always believed they would be able to veto the unpopular move following trials in five pilot areas.

Last week the government also sidelined parliament to move ahead with plans to introduce a controversial third runway at Heathrow airport.

The Tories discovered the bin tax measure in a little-noticed clause of the Climate Change Act. "New taxes are being imposed by arrogant and out-of-touch rulers, showing contempt for the democratic process. The imposition of extra-parliamentary taxation is a constitutional outrage," said Eric Pickles, shadow communities and local government secretary."

3. Select Committees

Legislation can be proposed by the executive in over twenty different areas of Government responsibility represented by the various Whitehall departments. No individual MP can be expert on all of the areas and able to monitor each of them. A system of Select Committees therefore exists to monitor each of the departments of state.

Unfortunately the structural intent of the Select Committees (other than the Select Committee on Public Accounts, see below) has been perverted by the party political system. The Members of the Committees and particularly the Chairs are now appointed by the whips of the respective parties. This means that the primary scrutiny system in the House of Commons has largely been neutralised as the Government normally has a majority of MPs on every Committee and these are most unlikely to support any report which is critical of the Government. In addition the full House of Commons is under no obligation to debate any of the reports produced by the Select Committees. In practice it is very rare that such reports are ever properly considered by other MPs or given a realistic response in the House of Commons by the Government departments concerned in a way which allows the response to be interrogated.

Select Committees have the power to call for evidence and many private sector organisations are very willing to provide their point of view to these committees. However the committees are unable to force any minister, civil servant or special adviser to appear before them. This is clearly unsatisfactory as it means that the Government is able to evade answering the questions that the Select Committee wishes to put to it. A simple solution would be to require any person paid for by the taxpayer to have to appear before a Select Committee just as it can require any other person to appear before it.

The Power Inquiry report published in February 2006 recognised the urgent need to strengthen scrutiny: *"Select Committees should be given independence and enhanced powers including the power to scrutinise and veto key Government appointments and to subpoena witnesses to appear and testify before them. This should include proper resourcing so that committees can fulfill their remit effectively."*

The Select Committees clearly need to be strengthened if Parliament is to provide any proper scrutiny of the executive. This should also be extended to reviewing proposed Government legislation prior to its coming before the full House of Commons for its first reading in order to improve the drafting of such laws and to identify the potential areas of contention (as is the practice in the Scottish Parliament). A further proper role for the Select Committees is to review all legislation after a period of, say, five years in order to see if the original justification for the legislation remains valid and whether there are any adjustments which are required.

The Better Government Initiative, chaired by Sir Christopher Foster, includes current and former senior civil servants and other interested participants in government and has stated in its report *Governing Well*:

> *"The capacity of Parliament to scrutinise the proposals of the Executive and to hold it to account for its decisions should be strengthened. Parliament should provide for more rigorous initial analysis of policy proposals and retrospective review, after a suitable period of time has elapsed, of the costs and outcomes of policy and legislation actually achieved against those in the initial proposals."*

In particular the Commons has minimal input to the crucial issue of public spending which is negotiated between the Treasury and individual departments without any real Parliamentary scrutiny. Nevil Johnson referred to this lack of scrutiny of expenditure by Parliament when he said in 1980: *"Its influence over proposals for expenditure is virtually nil and has been for decades. It has a marginal post-facto influence on spending procedures through the Public Accounts Committee, but all attempts to strengthen its position before financial commitments are given statutory force have failed."*

The Better Government Initiative has suggested:

- *On tax, there should be a genuine Green Budget, separating changes in tax rates from new taxes and providing draft clauses on new taxes, all reaching parliament at least as early as the present Pre-Budget Report and preferably earlier*

- *On expenditure, Parliament should be involved at an early stage in the broad issues of Comprehensive Spending reviews. In the annual process the relevant Select Committees should provide a commentary which the House would have when it considered the Executive's proposed plans for total spending and its allocation."*

The Select Committee on Public Accounts provides an example of how Select Committees could work as by tradition the Chair always comes from the Opposition. In addition it effectively has sufficient independent staff as its work is concentrated on reviewing the reports from the National Audit Office which is staffed by professional accountants and other experts who are not civil servants. Unlike the staff of other Select Committees they have full rights of access to departmental papers, records and interviews.

All Select Committees should be properly independent of the executive. The Jury Team Governance Proposal is therefore that the members of all Select Committees (using the way many committee members are elected in the City of London Common Council) should be chosen by a vote of the whole House of Commons rather then being appointed by the whips.

A secret ballot has now been introduced for the election of the Speaker and there is no reason why the same procedure should not be used for electing members of Select Committees.

> Members of Select Committees, which hold the executive to account, should be elected by all MPs and not appointed by party whips, and should scrutinise all departmental proposals for legislation.

F. Ensuring European Legislation is Appropriate

1. The Prevalence of European Legislation

It is estimated that over two thirds of new laws and regulations are linked to European Union directives. British people and businesses are fairly long suffering and will accept most regulations as part of the burden of living in a democratic society. However the area that most arouses their fury is when they perceive that under the cloak of European requirements the British Government legislates in a way that is significantly more onerous than is the case in other member states. This is encapsulated in the phrase *"the level playing field"*. Whether it is a much publicised prosecution of a cheese producer, the selling of apples by pounds or the regulations on road transport, it is the inequity of the British approach which generates the headlines.

EU directives typically set out a minimum level of standards on the particular issue in a directive of a few pages. However the responsibility for citizen and consumer protection is that of individual Governments and therefore European directives have to be translated into national legislation.

UK Parliamentary time is scarce and it is difficult for departments to get more than a couple of legislative slots per year. The main opportunity for departmental initiatives is therefore through Statutory Instruments and the most fruitful reason for these is European directives.

2. Gold Plating

A particular UK concern is that of "gold plating" which is where the UK goes beyond the minimum required by a European directive in promulgating a UK regulation whose basis is that directive. In the UK the authority for making such regulations derives from Section 2(2) of the European Communities Act 1972. This Section authorises regulations to be made for the purpose of

- *"implementing any Community obligation of the United Kingdom",* or
- *"dealing with matters arising out of or related to any such obligation".*

This very broad power can be used to over-ride or amend existing Acts of Parliament and this machinery to amend the law is very attractive to officials since the Statutory Instrument procedure is subject to much less Parliamentary scrutiny than a Bill. Therefore the use of regulations under Section 2(2) of the 1972 Act has ballooned enormously over the years and many important or controversial changes to the law are made by this route.

The vastly increased use of section 2(2) to make important changes to domestic law makes a mockery of the assurances which were given to the House of Commons by the Government in the course of the debates on the 1972 Act, when it was said that any important changes would be made by Bill rather than by subordinate legislation.

For example, Geoffrey Rippon in the second reading debate, Hansard 15th February 1972 column 282, said: *"I fully appreciate the concern of the House at any new general power to make subordinate legislation, but I should like to reassure Hon. Members about the prospect. On the basis of existing Community instruments, we foresee a need for not more than four instruments under clause 2(2) in 1972 and about another 12 in 1973."*

Since then there have been more than 15,000 uses of clause 2(2).

3. The Inadequate Scrutiny of European Legislation

These regulations and other EU matters are meant to be reviewed in the Commons by a special Select Committee called the European Scrutiny Committee. However the Committee does not have the power to take any substantive votes. The Committee itself described its role as solely *"sifting EU documents on behalf of the House".* It deliberates in secret, except when interviewing ministers and other non-members and this makes it harder for other MPs and the general public to know what is happening. Even if a proposed document is referred to one of the three European Standing Committees then this is likely to have little EU expertise and usually a low attendance.

In a 2004 Review, the then Leader of the House Peter Hain admitted, *"The European Standing Committees have not worked out as it was hoped. It is hard to persuade Members to serve on them. Few other Members think them worth attending. Their proceedings have a ritualistic quality, and are largely devoid of much political interest; yet they consume a lot of time and effort. There is a very strong case for reform."* However there has been no significant reform.

Peter Hain also commented: *"Our national Parliament is very ignorant about the European Union, save for a small group on the Scrutiny Committee who know everything. Indeed, they know far too much. They talk in their own language and the rest of the MPs know virtually nothing about the EU."*

Michael Gove, a Conservative MP, now Shadow Secretary of State for Children, Schools and Families and a member of the House of Commons EU Scrutiny Committee, has said: *"The current system allows the Government to sign up to EU legislation in meetings in Brussels, without first having sought agreement from Parliament. Often Parliament isn't even given time to discuss the issues. In fact even when Parliament specifically asks the Government for time to debate a new EU law, the Government increasingly chooses to use the so-called 'override' mechanism to avoid Parliamentary scrutiny."*

Since 2001 when the figures were first collated, this 'override' has been used over 350 times to pass EU legislation without proper scrutiny in Parliament. The Government has claimed that this is necessary to avoid undue delays. However it is interesting to note that the Government used the override 22 times in 2005 during its own presidency of the EU when it controlled the agenda itself. Particularly controversial uses of the override have been to create the EU Arrest Warrant and to set up the European Defence Agency.

Currently the EU produces around four pieces of secondary legislation each week, which means that with the UK Parliament not sitting for more than half of the days in the year, there is more than one new piece of EU legislation every Parliamentary day. There is also a great deal of other documentation coming from Brussels which can affect UK citizens or businesses. In total about 1,200 documents a year are classed as EU ones and subject to scrutiny (more than seven per Parliamentary day). Parliament is in complete recess for around 16 weeks a year, whereas the European Commission only shuts down for August. According to a Parliamentary written answer, in 2005 alone there were 68 occasions where the Council of Ministers adopted proposals which had not been reviewed by the Scrutiny Committee because the House of Commons was in recess (or was prorogued for the general election).

It is therefore proposed that the European Scrutiny Committee be reformed so that it can publicly review all proposed EU legislation before it is enacted and each departmental Select Committee be given the power to recommend agreement or rejection as appropriate of each Statutory Instrument to ensure that it is not being used for any purpose not required by the original EU directive.

> No European directive should be enacted or enforced by secondary legislation in a stricter way than is the practice in any other European country deemed compliant for that directive by the European Commission.

G. Limiting the Term for MPs

1. The Relationship of Parliament and Government

Parliament should limit the power of the executive but should not be the vehicle for Government. J. S. Mill wrote that:

"There is a radical distinction between controlling the business of Government and actually doing it".

Similarly Prime Minister Gladstone said to the House of Commons:

"Your business is not to govern the country, but it is, if you think fit, to call to account those who do govern it."

Parliament should therefore act in a similar way to the trustees of a charity or the non-executive directors of a major company. The Government is equivalent to the management of a charity or company which undertakes the detailed implementation of the agreed strategy. A key role of the trustees or non-executive directors is to review this implementation to see whether it is being done ethically, effectively, efficiently ad economically and in order to do this they must maintain sufficient independence to be able properly to review the proposals and actions of management.

It is vital that people are attracted to Parliament as part of their career, and not as their main career, so that they can maintain their independence.

2. Current Practice in the Length of MPs Careers

There are no term limits for MPs which would be a way of ensuring that MPs do not become too comfortable with their lifestyle and too separate from the rest of the population. Most US states now have such term limit legislation which also applies to the US President and the equivalent in many other countries. Without such term limits MPs are less likely to give priority to legislation or scrutiny as the job of being an MP becomes a career in itself.

At the 2005 election the Labour MP Tam Dalyell retired after 43 years and the Conservative Sir Teddy Taylor retired after 40 years. After the 2005 election, Sir Peter Tapsell continued to serve after 44 years in the House and Alan Williams was also still there after being first elected in 1964. Two other MPs had been elected in the 1960s, 37 in the 1970s and 104 in the 1980s.

Assuming that the next general election is held in 2010, two thirds of MPs will have served for more than 13 years, 38% for more than 18 years and 23% for more than 23 years, hugely longer than is allowed under any other independent scrutiny model permitted in the UK.

3. Term Limit Principles

Term limits are well established in the charitable and private sector. Trustees are not allowed to have any conflict of interest with their organisation or to receive any benefits from it. Similarly all major company boards should now have a majority of non-executive directors who, although paid a fixed fee, are not allowed to receive any other benefits from the company.

In particular it has been recognised that trustees and directors can lose their independence if they serve on the board for too long. The Charity Commission sets out clear guidelines on this. Similarly for public companies directors are normally elected for a period of three years and are not normally re-elected for more than three periods of three years, a total of nine years. If there are special reasons why a company wants a particular director to continue on the Board for more than nine years then that person is subject to a vote by shareholders every year instead of every three years.

In Government the agreed strategy is provided by the framework of legislation. Government departments and agencies then implement this. It is Parliament which is responsible for holding the Government to account. Unfortunately Parliament has ignored all of the corporate governance improvements it has required for other institutions in the country. There are clearly many continual influences by the executive on MPs from potential appointments to eventual seats in the House of Lords.

The Jury Team therefore proposes term limits for MPs (if there are any particular people whose time as an MP comes to an end as a result but the Prime Minister still wants them to serve in the Government, then they could be appointed to the House of Lords). The Jury Team Governance Proposals therefore include:

MPs should normally serve for no more than three full terms.

H. Stabilising the Length of Parliaments

1. The Statutory Background

In 1715 as part of the readjustment of responsibility between the monarch and the politicians the House of Commons negotiated that the maximum length of a Parliament would be extended to seven years. Although that was reduced to five years in 1911 as part of the Parliament Act, the power of the Prime Minister, acting by use of the Royal Prerogative, to dissolve Parliament within this maximum period has never been addressed by statute.

Noting this, the 1992 Labour Manifesto pledged *"Although an earlier election will sometimes be necessary, we will introduce in general a fixed Parliamentary term."* However it did not make any such pledge in its 1997, 2001 or 2005 Manifestos when it could sense power or was in power.

Parliament is limited to five years but elections are typically held every four to five years. The power of the Prime Minister, based on the Royal Prerogative, to decide when within the five years the election should be held is a very powerful one, especially now that opinion polls tend to be broadly correct. It is usually exercised when the incumbent sees the maximum electoral advantage for their own political party rather than for the country as a whole.

2. The Effect of an Uncertain Parliamentary Term

The agreed maximum length of a UK Parliament of five years is a good planning period during which a Government should be able to implement a substantial proportion of its policies. This is slightly more than the four year US Presidential cycle but less than the seven year French Presidential term.

As well as giving a political advantage to the incumbent prime minister, the uncertainty about when a general election may occur means that a lot of Parliamentary activity can be wasted as bills which have not completed all of their stages have to start again from the beginning in the new Parliament. In addition enquiries by committees stop and their reports are not published.

The uncertainty about the length of a Parliament also affects the management of all of the departments of state. Senior civil servants do not know how much effort to put into a particular policy if at an uncertain date a new Government may be elected with a different policy. This leads to inefficiency.

The Independent commented in July 2008:

> *"The prospect of an election means a desperate expediency will prevail – imprudence for a purpose. The Chancellor plays a reluctant Santa Claus in order to keep his fearful MPs in marginal seats happy, or less frightened. He buys a very short-term happiness."*

For these reasons other Westminster style Parliaments such as those in Australia, Canada, India and New Zealand all have fixed terms as does the United States. In Germany the Bundestag may only be dissolved prematurely in exceptional circumstances. Similarly the Scottish Parliament, the National Assembly in Wales, the Northern Island Assembly and all other elected bodies in the UK have fixed terms of office, normally four years.

3. The Role of the House of Commons

The only reason why elections have been called at a time not of the choosing of the Prime Minister has been when the governing party has lost a vote of confidence in the House of Commons. This is however very unusual and last happened in 1979.

This should clearly remain as a sanction on the Government but other than this there is no reason for the benefit of the country, rather than for his or her political party, why the Prime Minister unilaterally should be able to dissolve Parliament using the Royal Prerogative and therefore call an election to try to get another term for him or herself.

Currently a motion of "No Confidence" passed by the House of Commons will lead to a general election. However the House of Commons conversely has no way of stopping a Prime Minister from calling an election. It is proposed that this position be reversed with there being an assumption that a Parliament will last for five years unless there is a House of Commons motion reducing this.

According to a ComRes survey of 154 MPs conducted in October 2007, 44% of MPs support fixed-term parliaments and 49% oppose them (support from 88% of Liberal Democrat MPs, 41% of Labour MPs and 25% of Tory MPs).

It is proposed that general elections should only be held every five years unless there is a resolution of the House of Commons that a general election be called, taking this discretion away from the Prime Minister.

> General elections will take place every five years unless a resolution of the House of Commons decides otherwise to reduce this period

I. Introducing Referendums

"The instant the people allows itself to be represented, it loses its freedom".
~ Jean-Jacques Rousseau

1. Guarding the Guardians

Even when we have independent MPs and the other improvements described above, a rounded political system requires that the people can also directly express their view on particular issues between elections. A properly representative House of Commons would be a much better determinant of political decisions than the current one. However even that would not have total legitimacy in the modern world. It is therefore important that citizens have the right through initiatives to call for a referendum on key issues to provide more of a check on political decisions other than just through a national vote every few years. This also limits the power of the Government.

Quis custodiat ipsos custodies? (Who will guard the guardians?)
~ Juvenal, the 1st/2nd Century Roman poet

We need to ensure that responsible citizens feel connected with the process of running the country in an increasingly complex world. As well as arranging for the best people to go into Parliament and Government, it is important that beyond this there is also a proper and coherent way for the people to adjust the laws which are made.

2. Support for Referendums

Patrick Dunleavy showed in his book *Voices of the People* that there is huge support by the public for the use of referendums. When asked the question *"Should the Government decide all important issues, or should Britain adopt a referendum system whereby certain issues are put to the people to decide by popular vote?"* 77% said they wanted a referendum system and only 19% wanted the Government to be left to decide. This 1995 poll also found that 77% of people thought that it was a "*good idea*" that if a petition were signed by "*say a million people*" the Government should be required to hold a referendum.

The Jury Team recently organised a question on referendums as part of the YouGov poll referred to in the Introduction section of this book. (Total sample size was 2161 adults. Fieldwork was undertaken between 30th Jan - 2nd Feb 2009. The survey was carried out online. The figures have been weighted and are representative of all GB adults).

Respondents were asked: *"Please imagine that there was a proposal that British people could force the government to hold a referendum on a particular issue by raising a petition with signatures from, say, a million people. Do you think this proposal is?".*

	Total	Male	Female
A good idea	**70%**	**69%**	**71%**
A bad idea	15%	20%	10%
Don't know	8%	5%	11%
Neither	7%	7%	8%

These results show that 70% think that a citizens' initiative for a referendum is a good idea and an analysis by age range shows support from all generations with the greater support from the older groups:

	18 to 24	25 to 34	35 to 44	45 to 54	55 +
A good idea	**65%**	**66%**	**69%**	**71%**	**74%**
A bad idea	16%	16%	13%	14%	15%
Don't know	9%	11%	8%	7%	6%
Neither	10%	7%	10%	8%	5%

There was overwhelming support from all parts of the political spectrum:

	Lab	Con	Lib Dem	Others	None	Don't know
A good idea	**67%**	**79%**	**61%**	**72%**	**70%**	**66%**
A bad idea	19%	11%	18%	13%	13%	2%
Don't know	8%	5%	9%	6%	9%	22%
Neither	7%	6%	12%	8%	8%	10%

The Economist clearly described this when it stated:

"As the old differences of wealth, education and social condition blur, it will be increasingly hard to go on persuading people that most of them are fit only to put a tick on the ballot paper every few years, and that the handful of men and women they thereby send to Parliament must be left to take all the other decisions"

The Conservatives Lord Salisbury, Arthur Balfour, Stanley Baldwin and Winston Churchill all called for referendums. The Conservatives proposed a referendum over reform of the House of Lords in the early 1900s, over Irish Home Rule between 1910 and 1914, and about trade and Imperial preference in 1930. In 1945 Winston Churchill proposed a referendum on the continuation of the wartime coalition until the defeat of Japan although this was rejected by Labour's leader, Attlee, who probably saw his chance at power as soon as the election could be held.

In 1910 in the House of Lords, approving of the idea for a referendum about Irish Home Rule, the Conservative Lord Curzon stated that the referendum is:

"essentially democratic in its character. Its basis is the belief, to which we all, on both sides of the House, give expression in our public utterances, that in the last resort we accept the will of the people, and I am at a loss to understand why, when it is put forward in this proposal, it should be greeted with so much doubt and, apparently, with so much dismay by those who profess to be the real representatives of the democracy in this country".

Balfour, a Conservative ex-leader and Prime Minister, said in the same debates:

"The referendum, at all events, has this enormous advantage that it does isolate one problem from the complex questions connected with keeping a Government in office, and with other measures which it wants to carry out and with other questions of foreign and domestic policy. It asks the country not 'do you say that this or that body of men should hold the reins of office?' but, 'do you approve of this or that way of dealing with a great question in which you are interested?' "

The End Of The Party

Theodore Roosevelt said. *"The majority of plain people will, day in and day out, make fewer mistakes in governing themselves than another smaller body of men will make in trying to govern them."* Similarly, Niccolò Machiavelli said that the multitude will on the whole be as wise as or wiser than Princes.

In his speech to the Campaign for Freedom of Information's Annual Awards ceremony in March 1996, Tony Blair said.

"The crucial question is does the Government regard people's involvement in politics as being restricted to periodic elections? Or, does it regard itself as in some sense in a genuine partnership with people? And the Government's attitude to what it is prepared to tell people and the knowledge it will share with them says a great deal about where it stands on that matter.

My argument is that if a Government is genuine about wanting a partnership with the people who it is governing, then the act of Government itself must be seen in some sense as a shared responsibility and the Government has to empower the people and give them a say in how that politics is conducted."

Zac Goldsmith, a Conservative candidate, wrote in The Sunday Times in September 2008:

"In the sense that we, the people, still have the right to remove our government once every few years, Britain is a democracy. But I believe the time has come to acknowledge that our current form of democracy is too crude and inadequate to serve properly a sophisticated 21st-century society.

People are switching off, not out of apathy but from a conviction that their voice is not being listened to. 'They're all the same' is a commonly heard lament - and people are increasingly resorting to voting for fringe parties such as the BNP, whose policies and agendas would be disastrous for Britain.

Yet there is a solution: a simple mechanism that, if made an integral part of the democratic process, could both improve the quality of decision-making at national and local levels and restore the public's faith in politics. That mechanism is the referendum.

The public longs for a greater role in decision-making but has little expectation that this can be achieved. Instead, as a nation, we are becoming ever more sullen and mutinous. Eventually MPs and councillors will come to understand that only by sharing power with their fellow citizens through a proper system of direct democracy will they recover the goodwill and respect that were once theirs by right."

3. The Use of Referendums by the Government

Referendums have recently been proposed on questions as widely divergent as continuing membership of the European Union or as to whether a particular town should have an elected mayor. Each of these referendums (other than local ones for mayors) has however been proposed to take place at a time of choosing of the Government of the day, normally in order to neutralise a difficult party political situation.

The only nationwide UK referendum has been the 1975 one about continuing membership of the EEC which followed Labour's 1974 general election Manifesto pledge for a referendum. Seven of the twenty-three members of the Labour Cabinet opposed EEC membership in the referendum campaign and at a special one day Labour Party conference on 26 April 1975, the Labour membership rejected continuing EEC membership by almost 2:1. Despite this the Government officially endorsed the "*Yes*" campaign and Harold Wilson said *"'Her Majesty's Government have decided to recommend to the British people to vote for staying in the Community".* A pamphlet was sent *"to every household in Britain"*, the purpose of which was to "*help you to decide how to cast your vote*" and to "*ask you to vote in favour of remaining in the Community*". The "*Yes*" campaign was also supported by the majority of the Conservative Party and by its newly-elected leader Margaret Thatcher. Vernon Bogdanor said in 1981:

"The EEC referendum ... encouraged a sense of social unity by enabling some political activists to reach out across party lines and establish contact with those holding similar opinions on the EEC but widely differing opinions on other political issues ... The EEC referendum seemed to bring out a sense of public spirit which had barely been tapped by the political parties."

There have been referendums at a sub-national level such as in Northern Ireland in 1973, about whether Northern Ireland should remain part of the UK or join the Republic of Ireland, and in 1998 on the Good Friday agreement. Referendums were used in 1979 in relation to devolution in Scotland and Wales, producing a negative result. Following the Labour Party's return to Government in 1997, White Papers were published again setting out proposals for devolution. Referendums were held in Scotland and Wales in 1998 and won, very narrowly in the case of Wales. Referendums have also been used to determine such issues as whether alcohol should be sold in areas of Wales.

John Prescott, Deputy Prime Minister, identified what he believed was the apparently unfair extra funding of Scotland compared with Northern England and this led to his championing of the idea of English regional assemblies which could then become part of the Scottish "Barnett" formula. Labour's 1997 Manifesto set out the prospect for regional devolution in England where there was "*demand*". The Government organised a consultation exercise in all the regions of England to determine the level of interest in holding a referendum about an elected assembly. This was generally described as "*cosmetic*". Prescott tried to engineer a positive position by arranging that the referendum on an assembly in the North East be conducted with an all postal ballot. The North East referendum however clearly demonstrated the will of the people with 78% voting against a regional elected assembly. The Government's policy of creating English regional assemblies was therefore changed completely by its overwhelming defeat in this referendum.

The Blair Government established procedures for there to be local referendums on having an elected mayor in areas of England and for the first time allowed these to be based on a popular initiative with there having to be such a referendum if one in 20 electors (5%) asked for it. About 30 such referendums have been held but with only about one third of them leading to approval for an elected mayor. In order to encourage more referendums on this issue the Government has now proposed that the threshold be reduced from 5% to only 2%.

In February 2009 the Conservative Party announced that they would support the idea of referendums at local government level if requested by 5% of the electorate if an increase in council tax broke a certain threshold. However they remain opposed to any similar system at national level.

4. Labour Party Proposals on National Constitutional Change

In the last 10 years the Labour Party Manifestos promised three national referendums to decide on:

- electoral reform
- the adoption of the Euro
- the new EU Constitution

but none of these has taken place.

The 1997 Labour Manifesto included the explicit pledge *"we are committed to a referendum on the voting system for the House of Commons. An independent commission on voting systems will be appointed early to recommend a proportional alternative to the first past the post system."*

The Jenkins Commission was duly appointed and it reported in October 1998 recommending that the first past the post system be maintained but with larger sized constituencies and using the Alternative Vote System so that all members were elected by a majority of the votes cast. It also said that there should be a number of other seats which would be allocated on party lines to make the arithmetic in Parliament represent the total votes. However despite this clear Labour Manifesto pledge no action has been taken by the Government on the Jenkins report.

The 2001 Manifesto also promised an assessment of the working of the different electoral systems that had been installed in Scotland and Wales and for mayoral elections since 1997. However the Government did nothing substantive towards this. The 2005 Labour Manifesto was even more watered down. It promised to review the existing electoral systems and then vaguely stated that a referendum "*remains the right way to agree any change for Westminster*" but it did not promise actually to hold such a referendum.

The Labour Party was also very two-sided about the case for a referendum on the new European Constitution/Lisbon Treaty. The Minister for Europe, Peter Hain, said the constitution was *"just a tidying up exercise"* whereas the Prime Minister said it was *"absolutely fundamental ... more important than Iraq"*. Rod Liddle reported Peter Hain's varying views on the issue in an article in The Sunday Times in June 2008:

> *"As Peter Hain, put it, when he was leader of the House: "This is not a major change - there's no need for a referendum." All clear? But then later he said: "I am not saying it has got no substantial constitutional significance ... of course it will have." And finally he said of the treaty (to the Financial Times): "Our task is nothing less than the creation of a new constitutional order for a new united Europe." All things to all men, Peter Hain - but he was not alone."*

Similarly Tony Blair himself took four different positions. In 1997 he wrote, *"If there are further steps to European integration, the people should have their say at a general election or in a referendum."* In 2003 he claimed to see *"no case for having a referendum on the new EU Constitution".* In 2004 he announced that there would be a referendum on the EU Constitution. In 2005 he said there would not be a referendum on the Lisbon Treaty.

When the Lisbon Treaty came to a vote in the House of Commons, the Liberal Democrat leader, Nick Clegg, said he agreed with the Government that the Treaty was "*a rather different beast*" to the Constitution and therefore a referendum was not necessary. However he said that there should instead be a national poll on Britain's continued membership of the EU. He told the BBC Radio 4's Today programme: "*We would support the Government by not voting for a referendum. We would vote against a referendum on the treaty and vote in accordance with our long-held position that the real referendum that needs to be had is whether we stay in the EU or not.*"

There is an interesting current situation with the idea of a referendum on whether or not the UK should stay in the EU. Both the Labour and Conservative parties still have internal divisions on this but the Liberal Democrats have a clear view that the UK should stay in and UKIP have a clear view that the UK should leave. The Liberal Democrats and UKIP are however both united in wanting to have a referendum on this EU question. Although they take opposite views of the desired outcome they both support the holding of such a referendum. In the 2004 EU elections the

Liberal Democrats and UKIP together obtained 30% of the vote and 31% of the seats.

5. The Deficiencies of Solely Government Initiated Referendums

The above analysis of the Lisbon Treaty/EU Constitution debate shows how the political elites bat the idea of a referendum back and forth in line with their own self-centred perception of their political advantage. This demonstrates graphically the problem of it being only Government which can initiate a referendum. This is despite the fact that in this particular case a survey showed that 83% of the people wanted the referendum on the Lisbon Treaty which they believed had been promised to them in the 2005 Labour Manifesto in relation to the new EU Constitution. This was also in the context that there have been referendums in a number of other EU countries with notably the Irish being required by their constitution to have a referendum in which they then voted against the Lisbon Treaty.

Despite this the idea of a national referendum initiated by the people is still completely abhorrent to many of the Political Class who cite the importance of "*Parliamentary sovereignty*". The main political parties remain against the idea of citizens being able to initiate a national referendum as they see this as reducing their power.

For instance during the debate on the Lisbon Treaty in the House of Commons in 2007, the Conservative MP, Ken Clarke, a former Chancellor, said: *"It worries me that members of the political ruling class of this country have now lost their self-confidence and their ability to rely on their legitimacy as Parliamentarians to such an extent that no one among them dares defy the media, the hard-line Eurosceptics or any other people who demand a referendum, because they find themselves faced with a Parliamentary majority that they seek to overturn."*

> The first web response to this was posted by "AlanofEngland" who said: *"Well, Mr Clarke, as the song goes 'the times they are a changing'. I note the use of referenda by this Government when it suited them, we all know what they are. I see how referenda are used so well in Switzerland, and I don't think they are awash with*

corrupt politicians, as we are. We now need this tool to balance the lies of our elite political class."

"Andrew Hemsted" posted the additional comment: *"I think Ken should think that in the past we had more faith in our elected representatives to be more independent and less like career politicians to actually listen to what the public want. At present we seem to be drifting towards a culture where our MPs have no idea how the rest of the country thinks and feels, hence us wanting a referendum."*

As described above, there are many examples of the way in which UK Governments have tried to manipulate referendums. Even Ken Clarke recognised the problems of having only Governments decide when a referendum should take place when he said: *"The origin of referendums lies with people such as Napoleon and Mussolini. They were populist people who wished to override their Parliamentary institutions and to appeal to the people on carefully chosen issues."*

However referendums do not have to be only initiated by Governments and can be, and are, initiated by citizens in a wide range of jurisdictions around the world.

A substantial possibility of a hung Parliament after the next general election means that both the Conservative and Labour parties now need to seek support from Liberal Democrat voters. David Cameron has already done this very overtly with his emphasis on environmental issues with *"vote blue get green"* and even using the phrase that he is a *"liberal Conservative"*.

Labour said in its 1997 Manifesto that it would have a referendum on proportional representation as a key part of its appeal to Liberal Democrat voters. If the Labour Party continues to have a weak electoral position then it is very likely that it will again seek to find ways of specifically increasing its appeal on Liberal Democrat issues and this could well include again offering to have a referendum on the "Jenkins Commission" proposals. If this were to be so then it will be a further example of a referendum being used for party political advantage.

Michael Wills, the minister responsible for constitutional reform, has already raised this possibility when he praised the Australian

Alternative Vote (AV) system. He told a seminar by the Progress think-tank that the Government was prepared to be flexible on electoral reform and wanted it to form part of a national debate on constitutional change. Voting reform would not be introduced before the next general election but it could form part of an agreement between Labour and the Liberal Democrats in the event of a hung parliament.

6. The Case for a Citizens' Initiative

It is clear that referendums whose content and time is chosen by the Government are merely extensions of oligarchical politics that are used when the party political system completely breaks down. The ability to have a referendum should not just be left to the Government of the day for its own political purposes. It should either be formally mandated, as in Ireland where a referendum is required whenever the constitution is to be changed, or it should be triggered by the people if sufficient of them want to question a Government policy.

J. S. Mill, possibly without knowing it, foreshadowed the idea of the citizens' initiative for a referendum when he said that the ideal of representation is:

> *"This ultimate power they must possess in all its completeness. They must be masters, when they please, of all the operations of Government."*

Referendums allow specific issues to be extricated from a broad set of party agendas. An initiative allows a specified percentage of the electorate to require a referendum to be held.

Referendums also increase interest in politics. They are a legitimate way of demonstrating support for a particular point of view, an official version of signing a petition, an action in which four fifths of the population has participated. There is evidence from around the world that they increase turnout and voter interest in the political system.

People who believe in a particular issue want it to be properly debated and usually believe that their fellow citizens will support them. They therefore very much favour referendums which can deal with individual issues, rather than elections which cannot.

They feel it is much better to put their effort into single issue campaign activity or to participate in lobbying groups and similar movements, all of which are showing an increase in the major democracies.

This use of a citizens' initiative to implement a referendum is now accepted in about half of the states in the US and both at the canton level and nationally in Switzerland. In the US the idea of citizen initiatives arose because of the growth of the influence of interest groups and the "party machine" on the process of representative Government which the founding fathers had established. As is now the case in the UK, the US legislatures had been perverted away from the democratic ideals of independent representatives which their constitutional structures assumed. Woodrow Wilson stated:

"It must be remembered that we are contrasting the operation of the initiative and the referendum, not with the representative Government which we possess in theory and which we have long persuaded ourselves that we possess in fact, but with the actual state of affairs, with legislative processes which are carried out in secret, responding to the impulse of subsidised machines, and carried through by men [the legislators] whose unhappiness it is to realise that they are not their own masters, but puppets in the game."

Switzerland has allowed its citizens to call for a referendum since 1848 and about 3% of Government bills have been challenged by a referendum at the request of a citizens' initiative. This means that most Government business can still be conducted through the Parliament. However the existence of this referendum process acts as a significant check on the politicians and their rhetoric.

This has been described as leading to a "negotiated democracy" on the basis that citizens might otherwise seek a referendum and therefore means that politicians are very much less prominent in Switzerland (the President of the Confederation rotates every year). Referendums also lead to citizens becoming more informed as they can have a direct say on the issues. Switzerland is a small country with minimal natural resources but its referendum system of Government has allowed it to develop efficiently with a very high level of civil support and involvement.

The referendum has now become much more familiar and accepted and indeed, as shown by opinion polls, desired in the UK. People will say that as there was a referendum on one particular issue such as devolution or mayoral representation, they would like to have a referendum on other issues. This will make it increasingly difficult for Governments to explain why this should not be the case.

The Number 10 website now accepts e-petitions, which are similar in concept to a citizens' initiative, and this may give an indication of the issues about which people are concerned. Recently the four most popular current e-petitions shown were as follows, with a remarkable number of people supporting each given that they must know that each of their votes will probably have very little effect:

- Scrap the planned vehicle tracking and road pricing policy (1,811,424 votes)

- Create a new public holiday, the National Remembrance Holiday to commemorate The Fallen and our Nation, with the holiday falling on the second Monday in November each year, the day after Remembrance Sunday. (531,377 votes)

- Allow the Red Arrows to Fly at the 2012 Olympics (502,594 votes)

- Reduce Fuel duty to bring fuel prices back to an acceptable level (304,634 votes)

A referendum is only likely to be called for by a group of citizens when they think that they will win it. However the result is not always obvious as has been shown by the recent French, Dutch and Irish referendums on Europe. In the 1975 UK referendum on the EEC, opinion polls were showing that a clear majority of the electorate wished to leave. However at the end of the campaign there had been a substantial shift in public opinion and the referendum was won by about two to one.

7. The Practicalities of Referendums

It is important to ensure that those voting in referendums are properly informed and that it is not possible for quirky results to take place. It is therefore suggested that a minimum of 5% of the relevant electorate may call for a referendum. All such referendums will be voted on at the same time during the year which would most logically be on the same day as the annual local authority elections in May/June (with a maximum of, say, four propositions each year, chosen as those with the most signatures, in order not to overwhelm the voters).

The wording of a referendum is clearly important. This would be the responsibility in the UK of the Electoral Commission under the Political Parties, Elections and Referendums Act 2000 (PPERA). This so far only requires the Government to consult the Electoral Commission on the wording of the question but could easily be strengthened to give the Electoral Commission the right to agree the question. The PPERA also provides a suitable structure for other issues relating to referendums such as expenses.

There are various formulae to ensure that sufficient members of the electorate are in favour of a referendum before it is passed. These criteria can include requiring a minimal proportion of the electorate to vote or alternatively requiring agreement from a particular proportion of the electorate rather than of those actually voting, as happened in the Scottish devolution election which was lost in 1979. There is also the issue that the vote may go one way because of the immediate political situation. In addition there has been the danger apparent with the EU Lisbon Treaty referendum in Ireland that huge pressure is being put on the Irish to have another referendum in order to try to achieve a "Yes" vote and therefore a formal mechanism is required to decide when there should be a further vote.

In the UK system, Parliament retains sovereignty, even if as in the case of devolution it establishes other ways of making decisions. It is therefore suggested that Parliament passes a law which would introduce the possibility of citizens' initiatives for referendums. The detailed provisions would be subject to consultation but, in order to allow a clear but cautious introduction as is appropriate with any constitutional change, they would probably be along the following lines:

- Any citizens wishing to have a question put to a referendum would have to seek the agreement of the Electoral

Commission that the proposed question stated the proposition fairly

- The proposed question could not lead to any discrimination or to the breaking of any international treaty obligations although it could require the UK to negotiate an exit from a treaty

- The proposers of the question would have to collect signatures, to be verified by the Electoral Commission, equivalent to at least 5% of the relevant electorate within a period of six months and by at least two months before the date of the referendum

- A referendum question requiring a change in the law would only be deemed to be passed if there is a turnout of at least 50% with 55% of those voting being in favour of it

- Following a favourable vote the Government would have six months in which to get appropriate implementing legislation through Parliament

- The law implementing a successful proposition could be challenged in the courts by any group which believed that the legislation did not properly and reasonably implement the referendum proposition, such action to be given priority in the High Court timetable

- If Parliament failed to pass appropriate legislation implementing the referendum proposition, or the courts determined that such legislation did not properly implement the proposition, there would be a further referendum vote on the same question the following year and if again passed by 55% of those voting with at least a 50% turnout the wording of the question would itself become law to be interpreted as appropriate by the courts on the same basis as the common law.

- If a proposition was not passed by 55% at either the first or second vote then no substantially similar proposition, as determined by the Electoral Commission, could be put to a referendum for a period of five years from the last of the votes.

A Governance Principle is therefore to support the introduction of referendums in the UK on all appropriate issues whenever a suitable proportion of the population desires this.

> Referendums should be called annually at all levels of Government whenever requested by 5% of the relevant electorate

J. **Improving Departmental Management**

1. The Purpose of Departmental Administration

The previous nine Jury Team Governance Proposals have dealt with the need to get better legislation enacted by a higher calibre and less conflicted group of MPs, together with giving the public a direct say. However a further key element of the political system is the management and administration of the laws which have been passed. The 6+ million people employed by the Government have the task of implementing this legislation whether in health, education, the armed forces, the emergency services, tax collection, social security or the many other tasks given to the Government machine by Parliament.

It is said that *"To every complex problem there is a simple solution......, but it is usually wrong".* The simple solutions of party political philosophy are insufficient for the complex problems now faced by the developed world. The *"devil is in the detail"* both of policy and especially of delivery as is known by anyone who has run a complex organisation such as Lord Sainsbury of Preston Candover who famously said *"retail is detail".*

It is essential that we have a steady but responsive system for running the Government machine which is led by the 20+ departments of state. Their administration oversees, allows or limits all of the administrative tasks which impact citizens such as the school choice available to a child, the health provision for an elderly relative, the combat equipment protection for those on active service, the management of immigration, investment in infrastructure or the way in which subsidies are managed.

Expect the best, Prepare for the worst.
~ Muhammad Ali Jinnah

Departments do not have as their prime purpose the development of ideology. They are there to administer the current laws. Butler said of Gaitskell (who served as Chancellor immediately before him): "*We both spoke the language of Keynes, but with different accents*".

Governments are largely judged on their managerial competence but short political timescales prevent the long term development of effective organisations. This was commented on by Peter Riddell in The Times in May 2008:

> *"He noted the analysis of Sir Antony Jay, co-author of Yes Minister, about how companies in trouble engage in selective panic and produce lots of little measures that result in chaos. This 'displacement activity for the disturbed', as Professor Hennessy calls it, has clearly been visible in Whitehall for the past six months, as Mr Brown has believed that the vitality of his Government is shown by unveiling masses of new initiatives, often to little effect."*

2. The Current Leadership of Departments

The Prime Minister is the person who can command majority support in the House of Commons. He or she then appoints ministers to oversee the departments of state. The function of departments is now technocratic-managerial as they are required to operate as efficiently and effectively as possible within the legal framework set down by Parliament.

Ministers are however not usually appointed by the Prime Minister for reasons of trying to achieve the best management and administration of the department. The normal purpose is party political convenience, whether to seek balance between left and right or north and south or to bring somebody into the tent rather than having them being difficult outside.

This often leads to ministers from very different ideological backgrounds succeeding each other and directing that completely different sets of priorities be followed by the department at which they have newly arrived. The appointment of ministers by

Downing Street is almost never because the Minister has any expertise in the particular activities of the department concerned.

In addition the senior minister in the department has little or no influence on which junior ministers will be appointed to serve under him or her as these appointments are made independently by the Prime Minister. Similarly ministers are moved from department to department, or are relegated to the back benches, almost entirely for reasons of party political presentation and image rather than because it will improve the operation of the relevant departments.

This erratic and unpredictable system leads to confused and ever changing management as each newly appointed minister brings to the department their own personal prejudices and policies. They seek to make their political mark in the comparatively short time that they will have in office, almost certainly a lesser time then it will take any of their initiatives fully to be implemented.

In the early Victorian era, ministers were equally drawn from the House of Lords and the House of Commons. However they are now predominantly professional MPs who increasingly have little experience of running any organisation. For instance the members of the first Blair Cabinet in 1997, although marketed as a fresh start, had spent an average of 18 previous years in Parliament with essentially no normal management responsibilities.

By the end of the Parliament in 2005 only six ministers survived from the original 1997 Cabinet of 22. These were Tony Blair, Gordon Brown, John Prescott, Margaret Beckett, Jack Straw and Alistair Darling. Only three are still in the Cabinet in 2009.

The speed with which ministers move can be seen from considering over the last 20 years the Secretaries of State for Work and Pensions (formerly Social Security) and for Education (now Children, Schools and Families), areas where careful and consistent long-term leadership is particularly important. However in the twenty year period 1988 to 2008 the Department of Work and Pensions and the Department of Education each had 11 Secretaries of State:

Work and Pensions	Education
John Moore (July 25, 1988 - July 23, 1989)	Kenneth Baker (May 21, 1986 - July 24, 1989)
Tony Newton (July 23, 1989 - April 10, 1992)	John MacGregor (July 24, 1989 - Nov 2, 1990)
Peter Lilley (April 10, 1992 - May 2, 1997)	Kenneth Clarke (Nov 2, 1990 - April 10, 1992)
Harriet Harman (May 3, 1997 - July 27, 1998)	John Patten (April 10, 1992 - July 20, 1994)
Alistair Darling (July 27, 1998 - May 29, 2002)	Gillian Shepherd (July 20, 1994 - May 2, 1997)
Andrew Smith (May 29, 2002 - Sep 8, 2004)	David Blunkett (May 2, 1997 - June 8, 2001)
Alan Johnson (Sep 8, 2004 - May 6, 2005)	Estelle Morris (June 8, 2001 - Oct 24, 2002)
David Blunkett (May 6, 2005 - Nov 2, 2005)	Charles Clarke (Oct 24, 2002 - Dec 15, 2004)
John Hutton (Nov 2, 2005 - June 27, 2007)	Ruth Kelly (Dec 15, 2004 - May 5, 2006)
Peter Hain (June 28, 2007 - Jan 24, 2008)	Alan Johnson (May 5, 2006 - June 27, 2007)
James Purnell (Jan 24, 2008 - present)	Ed Balls (June 28, 2007 - present)

The average incumbency of these 22 appointments was therefore less than 22 months each. Indeed if Peter Lilley's five years at Social Security and David Blunkett's four years at Education are removed, the average incumbency of the other 20 appointments was only 18 months. Four of the eleven Secretaries of State at Work and Pensions served for less than a year and five of the eleven Secretaries of State for Education for less than two years.

Moving ministers at this rate means that they cannot properly develop any significant policy agenda and then oversee its implementation in the complex world beyond Whitehall. The system benefits the political party in power rather than the children, workers and pensioners that it is meant to be serving.

3. The Consequences of the Numbers of Ministers

The UK has more Government ministers than almost any other country. The Cabinet Office website lists 119 "Ministers,

Government whips and spokespersons in the House of Lords" of which 76 are Ministers in the House of Commons and 19 are Ministers in the House of Lords (the other 24 are the whips: 16 in the Commons and 8 in the Lords).

As an example of the growth in ministerial numbers, following the split of the Department of Education and Skills in June 2007 into the new Department for Children, Schools and Families and the new Department for Innovation, Universities and Skills, there are now a total of ten ministers covering the Education brief (five at DCSF and five at DIUS).

At each of these departments, and at many others, five ministers are therefore in place all trying to have good ideas and to develop initiatives which they can announce, driving the civil service machine increasingly to short-term and desperate measures to deliver.

Matthew Parris described this in an article in The Times in July 2008:

"The Government is drowning in shallow water. Ministers flail around in an alphabet soup of piddling little initiatives. Each time the clock strikes, a new idea of breathtaking triviality is press-released. With the morning papers come endless "clear messages" "sent out", pointing in all directions and none. And in this frenzy of dots, nothing joins up. Seldom has so much activity combined to produce so dismal an impression of stalemate.

We could get the above into perspective if we had a philosophical string on which to thread these coloured beads. In its place, communications gurus assure vacant-minded ministers that, because an insatiable media machine of 24-hour rolling news must be fed, they've got to keep those initiatives - any initiatives - coming.

The truth is otherwise. From a confidently led party with a coherent political philosophy, quite long periods of calm inactivity, even silence, are perfectly well understood by the voters. Voters hear tone more than they count words and measures. Babbling and tinkering inspire the opposite of confidence: they look desperate."

In addition to the ten ministers at DCSF and DIUS, there are two Parliamentary Private Secretaries (PPSs) at each department. In total there are now 45 Government PPSs in the House of Commons.

Although not paid any salary other than as an MP, PPSs are expected to vote with the Government and cannot, for example, be a member of a Select Committee or table an amendment to a Government bill. The total of 137 MPs on the "payroll vote" in the House of Commons, being 76 Ministers and 16 Whips together with the 45 PPSs, make up 39% of all Labour MPs.

In Parliament this large number of appointments helps the party in power because it means that they are a substantial part of Parliament which is necessarily pledged to support the Government and it also increases the patronage options for the party leadership.

During a Conservative Opposition Day debate on the relationship between Parliament and the executive in July 2000, Charles Kennedy said that there were too many people on the payroll vote:

> *"Secondly, far too many people are on the payroll in the House. The Government are too big. There are too many Parliamentary private secretaries and too many people are beholden to the Executive interests of the day. Not enough Members feel free to express independent interests from a Back-Bench point of view. It is telling that there is a genuinely held respect and affection in this place for individuals in all parties, some of whom are described by the press as "maverick", some of whom are called "independently minded" and some "troublemakers". The truth is that we all know that most Members do not have either the guts or the opportunity to be like that because those who sit on the Treasury Bench and who control the Executive have far more power than is healthy for the House."*

In its report, *Strengthening Parliament*, the Norton Commission, established by William Hague when he was Leader of the

Conservative Party, recommended a reduction in the size of Government:

- *The size of the Cabinet should be capped at 20.*
- *The number of junior ministers should be capped at 50.*
- *There should be only one Parliamentary private secretary per department, responsible to the Cabinet minister.*

A similar view was expressed by the House of Commons Modernisation Committee in its June 2007 report entitled *Revitalising the Chamber:*

> *Another reform, which directly affects the relationship of backbench MPs with the Executive, relates to the number of MPs on the payroll vote. The Hansard Society has argued that the number of MPs on the payroll vote weakens Parliament's ability to carry out its collective functions and is a mechanism by which Government exercises a specific form of control. The Commission on Parliamentary Scrutiny recommend that each Government department should have only one Parliamentary Private Secretary (PPS), although it recognised that a few larger departments might require more than one. Nonetheless, it proposed that the number of PPSs should be significantly reduced.*

In the 1999/2000 session Iain Duncan Smith introduced a Private Member's Bill, *The Government Powers (Limitations) Bill* and John Bercow, another Conservative, introduced a similar Private Member's Bill in 2002/03. These Bills would have introduced an absolute limit of 82 Ministers, whether paid or not with not more than 63 being Ministers of State or Parliamentary Secretaries. They also introduced the concept that a Minister's appointment should lapse after a period of three months unless it had been approved by the relevant Select Committee of the House of Commons. Both Bills were dropped before Second Reading.

In June 2006, Jeremy Browne, the Liberal Democrat MP, introduced a Private Member's Bill entitled the *Ministerial and Other Salaries (Amendment) Bill*. The Bill similarly sought to reduce the maximum number of Ministerial salaries payable from 83 to 60 and the Bill was again dropped before Second Reading.

Despite the opportunities presented by these Private Member's Bills, the Government has taken no steps to curb its influence over Parliament by adopting any of these proposals.

Although ministers should have collective responsibility for the policies for which they are responsible, blind obedience to a party line cannot be in the interests of the country or of the MP's constituents. The hierarchy of responsibility for an MP who becomes a minister must still in voting be firstly for the benefit of the country as a whole, secondly for their constituents and only thirdly for the government.

Jury Team members of a government would be expected to vote independently according to their best judgment on all issues. However if they were in a position of responsibility as a minister in putting a proposal for regulation or legislation to Parliament for a vote then they would obviously be expected to vote for that option as it would clearly be wrong to submit a proposal to Parliament and then to oppose it.

It would be assumed that the members of the Cabinet would vote for all proposals put to Parliament as the Cabinet should take responsibility for the submission of all such proposals. However Junior Ministers would be assumed only to have a position of responsibility for the proposals put forward by their own department. This mirrors the position in life outside Parliament where people only have collective responsibility for the decisions of the Boards/Committees on which they actually sit. Junior Ministers and PPSs would therefore be free to vote as they saw fit on measures outside of their own department.

In the event that a Minister, whether at Cabinet level or at a more junior level, disagreed with a proposal put forward to Parliament by a Board of which he or she was a member then they would have to resign from the position which led to the clash.

These principles, which are how other parts of society work, would therefore mean that the payroll vote would become much less overwhelming of Parliament.

4. The Management of Departments

The basis for our system of Government administration was set out in the 1854 Northcote-Trevelyan report. The famous second paragraph stated:

"It may safely be asserted that, as matters now stand, the Government of the country could not be carried on without the aid of an efficient body of permanent officers, occupying a position duly subordinate to that of the ministers who are directly responsible to the Crown and to Parliament, yet possessing sufficient independence, character, ability and experience to be able to advise, assist, and to some extent, influence those who are from time to time set over them".

When the Northcote-Trevelyan report was published in 1854, the total employment of all central Government departments was around 40,000, the largest group being involved in tax collection. Civil servants administered very small departments and Government was only involved in comparatively simple and limited issues. Both Whitehall and Westminster were based on the culture and practice of the gentleman's club and the country house. However as Government expanded, J. D. Gregory commented that a Government department could no longer be seen as a *"small family party"* and was now like a *"large insurance office or, in times of stress, a central railway station on a bank holiday"*. More recently Peter Hennessy commented: *"The hierarchical chain became just too long for a ministry to be run on the private country house model."*

The 1968 Fulton Report began with the statement: *"The home civil service today is still fundamentally the product of the 19th-century philosophy of the Northcote-Trevelyan report".* With the further expansion of the state, by the mid-1970s it was clear that Government could not operate the many industries it had nationalised especially finding that it was lobbied to give more weight to the producer interest rather than to the consumer interest.

Since that time the state has been reduced in some ways through privatisation but as at the end of 2008 the UK Government employs 6 million people, over a fifth of all UK employees. There are 1.5 million in the health service, 1.4 million in education, 1.2

million in administration, 0.5 million in the armed forces and the police, 0.4 million in social care and 1.0 million in other public sector areas, now including financial services. This is the largest Government payroll since the 1970s.

The UK civil service is regarded as one of the least corrupt public service systems in the world. It has also managed to adapt to substantial changes over the last 20 years with such elements as the creation of "Next Steps" agencies, Freedom of Information and the erosion of the lifelong career path. The civil service is one of the key elements of the country, described by both Anthony Verrier, of the University of Essex, and Jim Hacker, of the BBC comedy series *Yes Minister,* as *"the permanent Government*".

5. Reconciling Leadership and Management

Anthony Seldon, Tony Blair's biographer, stated that the Prime Minister was *"much more interested in - and better at - politics then management"*. Blair himself admitted that he had to *"learn to be Prime Minister".* In 2001 Blair told his Cabinet Secretary Sir Richard Wilson that he had *"managed the Labour Party"* but Wilson replied that Blair *"never managed them, you merely led them. There's a big difference".*

Ministers leading departments should fulfill essentially not political but management roles. Their leadership needs to be sensitive to political considerations but must also provide steady management and continuity if the people in the organisations are to give of their best. Unfortunately the current combination of political interference in departments combined with senior civil service staff of a very different background and outlook means that UK Government outcomes are often internationally uncompetitive and sometimes stark in their failures.

John Reid MP, a former Home Secretary, who himself had eight ministerial jobs in ten years, stated:

"Our system is not fit for purpose. It is inadequate in terms of its scope."

The issues relating to the clash between the short-term ministerial political culture and the longer-term civil service management culture were graphically described by Sir John Bourn, the former

Comptroller and Auditor General in charge of the National Audit Office, in an article in The Financial Times in May 2007:

"The whole culture of the senior civil service needs to be changed. The top jobs should go to those who have successfully managed programmes and projects – in health, social welfare and taxation as well as in construction and defence. At the moment they are given to those best at helping their ministers to get through the political week.

Projects and programmes should be designed to produce good results. Too many schemes today are like the structures children build with toy bricks – unbalanced, constantly wobbling, complicated to shore up and only too likely to come tumbling down – as in the arrangements for child support, and in the recent ill thought-out schemes for capital gains tax and the taxation of non-domiciled residents, which had to be amended even before they were put into operation

The machinery of government is in constant turmoil – new departments and authorities being set up and older ones shut down or amalgamated. Such churning costs millions of pounds and is largely irrelevant to the programmes and projects that have to be implemented. It should be stopped."

The interaction of the civil servants with ministers was not considered in the Northcote-Trevelyan report. This has become a major dysfunction in the operation of the Government machine as ministers have increasingly shorter careers and have become more involved with defending their own political party than with progressing sound governance. This was brought to life in *Yes Minister* which has been attested to by Prime Ministers from Margaret Thatcher onwards as realistically portraying the view that many ministers are out of their depth with their departmental briefs and are mainly interested in the image which they can portray to the public and especially to their party leadership.

Peter Hennessy commented on how the Northcote-Trevelyan report had left a shadow over Government administration because of the unintended consequence of lifetime civil servants trying to administer departments which were theoretically the responsibility of increasingly short-term ministers. He said:

"Only when Trevelyan's ideal had been achieved for several decades did it become apparent to more than a handful that those with 'sufficient independence, character, ability and experience' would very often be in a position to do more, much more, than 'advise, assist and to some extent influence' ministers set over them."

On this divergence between the ability, background, culture and outlook of ministers and civil servants, Peter Hennessy continued:

"But if ministers are not top-flight themselves in intelligence, character and independence of spirit they are in constant danger of being overawed by the dozen to two dozen Northcote-Trevelyan types in their departments on whom they very largely rely for day-to-day survival and long-term succour. The seeds of Yes, Minister were planted in that second paragraph of the Northcote-Trevelyan Report".

Departmental governance has been further damaged in the last twenty years by the rise of the "special adviser" who is a political appointee normally working more closely with the minister then do any of the civil servants. The Prime Minister now has 18 of these and there are a further 48 working for other ministers. Their power and influence has also grown as shown most graphically by the fact that Jonathan Powell and Alistair Campbell in Tony Blair's office were specifically given the authority by Order in Council to give instructions to civil servants. The heritage, culture and experience of modern senior civil servants makes it increasingly difficult for them to stand up for proper and well thought out management processes against the normally short-term media imperatives of the combination of minister and special adviser.

All of these problems with ministerial appointments come back to the fact that they are based on party politics:

- As a result of the adversarial nature of the House of Commons the Prime Minister can only choose ministers from his own party which normally limits his choice to less than three-fifths of the available MPs (even if all were suitable for and interested in ministerial office). Similarly in the House of Lords he is limited to less than a third of its members.

- The Prime Minister makes ministerial appointments on a party political basis by trying to balance the various wings of the party and satisfying any potential areas of discontent without any real consideration of what is suitable for the department concerned.

- With only 20% of MPs having five or more years experience of management, most ministers have little idea how to run a department. Politics has now moved away from ideology towards delivery but most ministers have a background in media imagery rather than in policy implementation on the scale required at the Government level.

- Ministers are frequently reshuffled in order to give the appearance of action or renewal solely to boost party poll ratings rather than to improve the management of the departments. As was said by Caius Petronius, Roman Consul, in 66 A.D.:

  "We trained hard, but it seemed that every time we were beginning to form up into teams we would be reorganised. I was to learn later in life that we tend to meet any new situation by reorganising: and a wonderful method it can be for creating the illusion of progress, while producing confusion, inefficiency and demoralisation."

- As an extension of prime ministerial patronage and as a useful mechanism for ensuring Parliamentary loyalty within the party, the number of ministers and Parliamentary Private Secretaries has massively increased over the last four decades. This leads to hyper-activism by ministers wishing to impress and to consequent confusion within departments.

- With the increased importance of the media to party politics, ministers now give this much greater attention with their special advisers. These exacerbate party political differences, increase the prevalence of adversarial politics and make it even harder to find the best management solutions to the issues facing departments.

These factors demonstrate that the huge increase in Governmental involvement and the changes in society mean that what may have been right in the eyes of Northcote and Trevelyan in 1854 is no longer a way to run an effective society.

There have been many studies and reports confirming this since before the First World War. However there has been no improvement in the situation and no real change in the relationship between the Sir Humphreys and the Jim Hackers throughout that period. The key reason for this is because of the temporary nature of political appointment which means that ministers are not in office long enough, and are often overawed by their sudden elevation, to be able to do anything about the obvious problems.

6. The Modern Approach to Organisational Governance

Modern governance requires that people appointed to senior office have the appropriate credentials for the role with relevant experience and a suitable track record. Whether being appointed as a charity trustee or to run a major company there will be a careful process to choose the person with the best fit for the job. However as the structure of Westminster/Whitehall has been unchanged for over 150 years, the appointment of ministers does not normally relate either to their knowledge of management or to their experience of a particular department.

There is now only a small difference on the key issues between the stated intentions of the major parties and most of their policy statements relate to how they would "*better manage*" the particular issue. This focus on delivery however makes ministers into managers which is a function for which they are normally peculiarly unsuited with no training either formally or in terms of their previous career.

Minette Martin described this in The Sunday Times in July 2008:

> *"Government, particularly a dirigiste and micromanaging one like ours, is a matter of management. "Delivering on" depends on competent management. Yet, incredibly, almost no one in government has any experience of management at all. None of the present cabinet has experience of managing a large business. The supposedly heavy hitters Brown, Darling, Straw, Smith, Johnson, Hutton and Balls have no management experience at all, according to the TaxPayers' Alliance."*

It has to be recognised that both civil servants, as professional managers and increasingly with specific expertise, and ministers, as representatives of the democratic will of the people, each have their role to play. The key issue is however the brutal interface between the two groups with their hugely different backgrounds and agendas.

Organisations such as departments of state are only effective if they develop a culture which is responsive to their "customers". This culture has to be established by design rather than from the whim of a particular Secretary of State. In order for such a culture to become embedded the agreed strategy and purpose of the department in serving its customers must remain central and not be overshadowed or diverted by short-term party politically driven initiatives. Departments should be judged not on their published intentions but on their actual behaviour in effectively and efficiently delivering on their purpose.

Away from Westminster and Whitehall, the principles of governance have developed greatly since the 1850s when it was common for all organisations to appoint people on the basis of their family connections, their local city or county allegiance or as a result of the benefit of a conflict of interest. In both the charitable and the corporate sector the way in which organisations should best be led and managed has now hugely changed and is well established. It must be implemented within Government.

The dichotomy between civil servants and ministers is one which also occurs in other fields and mechanisms have therefore been developed to deal with this. It is now well recognised that corporate governance cannot allow a chief executive just to operate on their own if they are using other people's resources. Various structural checks and balances have therefore been developed.

For instance the Combined Code on Corporate Governance adopted by the London Stock Exchange requires that for larger companies *"at least half the board, excluding the chairman, should comprise non-executive directors determined by the board to be independent."*

In a charity the chief executive and his or her staff will normally be professionals who are very competent managers and who have substantial experience in the area which the charity addresses, just like civil servants. The way in which a charity chief executive is held to account is through having a board of charity trustees. Its members are there to provide their own background expertise which might be in the particular area of the charity's activities but also might be in legal, commercial, social or other relevant areas. This ensures an independent review of the chief executive's proposals and actions.

Charities are set up, like Government departments, for the public benefit. The well rehearsed charity model of governance is therefore the one, rather than that of companies, which is most appropriate for Government departments. The Board of a Government department should act like the trustees of a charity to ensure that the executive management is acting ethically, effectively, efficiently and economically in line with the agreed strategies and priorities, normally the laws which have been laid down by Parliament.

An essential difference between the current structure of a Government department and the way in which all other organisations are run is that the Secretary of State in a department is both chairman and chief executive. The idea that one person should fulfill both of these roles has been squeezed out of all other aspects of UK governance. In the charity sector it is illegal for the paid chief executive also to be the chairman (and under the Combined Code for companies it is only in exceptional circumstances that the two roles can be combined, this being the case for less than 1% of the top 500 companies in the country).

In order to bridge the gap between ministers and civil servants it is therefore key that fully responsible departmental Boards be established. They would consist of the ministers in the department plus independent Board members as described below. The Boards would be chaired by the Secretary of State. As chair, the Secretary of State would represent the Department externally, as happens with charities and companies, including answering questions in Parliament. The other ministers in the department would as appropriate represent the Board's views both in Parliament and elsewhere within their own sphere of responsibility. The Permanent Secretary (the senior civil servant) would normally attend as the chief executive together with any of his or her staff who were relevant to the particular discussion.

It is therefore proposed that rather than the Secretary of State being the legal persona of the Department this should change to being the Board of the department. It would be the Board rather than the individual minister, in line with the position in every charity, company and association in the country, who would have the authority to make any pronouncement on behalf of the Department, which the Secretary of State could then communicate. This would give much greater stability and continuity to management and would mean that even when ministers were reshuffled there would not necessarily be a substantial change in direction or priority.

All pronouncements and other policy matters would therefore be issued in the name of the Board rather than of the Secretary of State or of an individual junior minister. This would lead to a massive improvement in management and a reduction in spin.

The development of new legislation would be controlled, as now, by the network of Cabinet Committees reporting into the Cabinet itself. The membership of these would be solely of ministers, as currently. The proposals actually to be put to Parliament for new legislation in the Queen's Speech or by other routes would also be decided, as now, by the Cabinet

There would therefore be a clear distinction between the administration of current laws and regulations and the proposal of new ones. The departmental boards, with their independent directors, would be responsible for administering all of the existing framework. Proposals for new laws and regulations would have to be approved by the relevant Cabinet Committee consisting solely of ministers. The main check and balance on those proposals would of course be the independent Select Committees and other MPs in the House of Commons.

7. The Appointment of Independent Directors

The appointment of "non-executives" is well established in other parts of the public sector. For instance on the Monetary Policy Committee, which sets interest rates, there is the Governor of the Bank of England plus the two Deputy Governors, the Bank's Chief

Economist and the Executive Director for Markets together with four external members appointed directly by the Chancellor. The Monetary Policy Committee states that: *"The appointment of external members is designed to ensure that the MPC benefits from thinking and expertise in addition to that gained inside the Bank of England."*

Most other public bodies have a majority of non-executives on the board. This is the normal format of most NHS and school governing bodies with it being the board, rather than any individual person, which is the legal persona. Similarly many Government agencies, especially those whose credibility and independence is paramount, have a requirement for a majority of non-executive directors. For instance the United Kingdom Accreditation Service, the sole national accreditation body recognised by Government to assess, against internationally agreed standards, organisations that provide certification, testing, inspection and calibration services, has four executive directors and five non-executive directors. Similarly the statute governing the London Development Agency requires that at least half of the Board must have had the experience of running a business.

The appointment of outsiders is now also recognised in the so-called "Next Steps" agencies which employ over 70% of civil servants and some of which have budgets much larger than some departments. Their senior official is often appointed by competitive recruitment from outside the civil service and they frequently also have boards which are much more like those of charities and companies.

Given all of these precedents, there is no reason why departments of state should not follow the governance principles that they mandate for others.

Many departments have established supposed boards of management during the last few years. However these have purely an administrative role and look at matters such as budgets and headcount and do not have any real authority over policy. They are chaired by the Permanent Secretary and ministers are not present. They do not have any legal persona and are purely advisory in relation to departmental policy. Their advice is only very rarely critical as the members of the boards are mainly the senior civil servants who work together on a daily basis anyway.

They typically only have a minority of two or three non-executive directors who depend for their remuneration and status on the goodwill of the Department. The boards were a response to the need for better departmental governance but have been a serious disappointment to anyone who might optimistically have expected that they would change ministerial behaviour. For instance the Cabinet Office Board, which stands at the centre of the Whitehall machine, just has the following restricted remit.

- *To recommend a business plan and resource allocation, and strategy for achieving the Department's business objectives to ministers*
- *Monitor and improve the Department's performance against these*
- *Ensure that risks are identified and effectively managed*
- *Oversee the Better Cabinet Office programme*
- *Ensure that standards and values within the Cabinet Office support the aims of the Department, and good Government more generally*
- *Safeguard and enhance the Department's standards and values.*

Ministers have resisted any proposals to reduce their own power and to give this to less political boards. For instance given the constant change in direction in the National Health Service as a result of different ministerial initiatives there has been strong support by health professionals for the establishment of a Board of Health to oversee the NHS. However a Department of Health Permanent Secretary recently said privately that his Secretary of State did not want any such body as: *"He enjoys playing with his train set, especially as it is the biggest one in Whitehall"*. It is essential that we stop this *"toys for boys"* attitude by ministers to the administration of massive organisations.

The appointment and composition of the new departmental boards is therefore vital. In order to replicate the accepted model of governance in all other fields, there would need to be a number of independent directors, with the Combined Code requiring that they make up at least one third of the board and recommending that they should be around two thirds.

In order to ensure that this is achieved, it is proposed that six independent members would be appointed to each Departmental

Board. As established in both the corporate and charity worlds, each member would normally serve for up to three periods of three years in order to provide continuity over changes in Government and to ensure that there is a corporate memory on the board (subject to initial transitional arrangements during which the terms will be staggered so that two members retire each year). It is expected that the Boards will normally meet monthly and will consider all of the policy and administrative issues facing the department.

The proper and independent appointment of these directors is clearly key to their effectiveness. It would obviously not be sensible for the department itself to appoint the Board members (as currently happens with the ineffective departmental boards which currently exist). It is therefore proposed that for each department, building upon the UK's rich heritage of civil society, seven relevant NGOs will be designated by the Office of the Commissioner for Public Appointments, subject to Parliamentary approval, to form an appointments panel to select the independent Board members. These NGOs would represent consumer as well as producer interests for each department. Each year one of the seven organisations would stand down from the appointments panel (as determined by lot in the first six years) with a new one chosen by the Commissioner in its place. The NGOs would be paid a small fee for providing their panel member.

The appointment panels would each undertake an annual assessment of the workings of the Board with which they were involved and would review the attendance and contribution of each of the Board members in line with best practice in the charitable and commercial sectors. They would decide whether to reappoint a member after each three year term or whether to seek new applicants for the role. In extreme cases they would also have the power to remove a Board member.

The job roles to be members of the Board itself will be extensively advertised by the Commissioner for Public Appointments. The appointment panels, with suitable support from the Commissioner's staff, will then meet to select the Board members from those applicants.

The Commissioner for Public Appointments would consult widely on appropriate organisations to form the appointments panels.

However potential examples of suitable NGOs each to nominate one member of the seven person appointment panels, which in turn would interview and appoint applicants for Board membership, are:

- Department for International Development: Oxfam, World Wildlife Fund, Voluntary Service Overseas, Fair Trade Foundation, BOND (British Overseas NGOs for Development), Overseas Development Institute and the Institute of Development Engineering

- Ministry of Defence: Royal United Services Institute, International Institute for Strategic Studies, Royal British Legion, Royal National Lifeboat Institute, Defence Manufacturers Association, Defence Surveyors Association and the Public & Commercial Services Union

- Foreign and Commonwealth Office: Royal Institute of International Affairs, Royal Commonwealth Society, Royal African Society, Royal Asiatic Society, Middle East Association, British North American Research Association and The Anglo Latin American Foundation

- HM Treasury: Royal Economic Society, Chartered Institute of Public Finance and Accountancy, Chartered Institute of Taxation, Securities and Investment Institute, Joseph Rowntree Trust, Institute of Directors and the Consumers Association

- Home Office: Prison Reform Trust, Association of Chief Police Officers, Liberty, Childline, Mind, Crime Concern and Migration Watch UK

- Department of Health: Academy of Medical Royal Colleges, Royal College of Nursing, UNISON, Medical Protection Society, Mencap, Age Concern England and the Family Planning Association

- Department for Children, Schools and Families: Barnado's, National Confederation of Parent Teacher Associations, National Governors Association, NASUWT (National Association of Schoolmasters and Union of Women Teachers), National

Association of Head Teachers, Citizens Advice Bureau, and the Chartered Institute of Personnel and Development.

- Department for Culture, Media and Sport: National Trust, British Hospitality Association, Museums Association, Royal Television Society, Equity, British Olympic Association and UK Sport.

- Department for Environment, Food and Rural Affairs: Royal Society for the Protection of Birds, Royal Institute of Chartered Surveyors, National Farmers Union, Country Land and Business Association, Greenpeace, Food and Drink Federation and the British Marine Federation.

The Governance Proposals therefore include:

> Departments will be run by a Board chaired by the senior departmental minister but on which at least half of the directors would be appointed by a panel of designated NGOs and other stakeholders relevant to consumer and producer interests in that sector.

K. Reducing Spin and Deceptive Statistics

1. The Suspicion about Government Statistics

People need to believe their political leaders but Government credibility has been much reduced because of the spin culture. In a 2008 survey by the Office for National Statistics, only 36 per cent of people thought that official figures were "*generally accurate*". Meanwhile, a 2007 poll of trust in Government statistics by the European Commission ranked Britain 27th out of 27 countries. A poll also found that 57% disapproved of using "*spin doctors to manipulate the media*".

Government statistics in the UK have long had a reputation for spin. In the 1980s changes in the rules affecting entitlement to unemployment benefit led to charges that the Thatcher Government were fiddling the statistics. That controversy led to the inclusion of a pledge to create an independent statistical service in the Labour Party's 1997 Election Manifesto.

A Statistics Commission was set up in June 2000 *"to advise on the quality, quality assurance and priority setting for official statistics, and on the procedures designed to deliver statistical integrity, and to help ensure official statistics are trustworthy and responsive to public needs."* However it clearly did not amount to anything like *"an independent statistical service"*. Although it was independent of ministers it had no authority directly to influence any statistics and was solely involved in procedures. It made some good progress within its limited remit but public concern about statistical spin increased.

There continued to be many examples of ministers abusing official statistics. On the 11th September 2001, Stephen Byers' special adviser sent round an e-mail at the time of the 9/11 attacks in New York to say that it would be *"a very good day to get out anything we want to bury"*.

In 2003, the then Transport Secretary, Alistair Darling, issued a press release that read: *"Deaths and serious injuries fell by 35 per cent on roads where speed cameras have been in operation."* Darling went on to say: *"The report clearly shows speed cameras are working... This means that more lives can be saved and more injuries avoided."* However the suggestion that the drop in accidents was caused by the cameras was rubbished by most statisticians as all that had happened was that previous peaks in accidents had reverted to the median level (if there are an above average 20 car crashes in an area one year but the next year there are only the average of 14 then it is clearly suspect to claim the reason and then extrapolate to the whole country that there has been a 35% drop in car crashes). Figures go up and down all the time.

Another much-publicised case was when the Education Secretary, Alan Johnson, became involved in a row on spin with claims that his special advisers tried to bury the announcement of poor primary school test results. The then Statistics Commission demanded to see the e-mail traffic and this showed that civil servants in the Department for Education and Skills (DfES) were overruled when they said that these figures should not be released on the same day as GCSE results which it was known would be dominant in the media. Special advisers told officials that they "*positively want[ed]*" both sets of results to be released at the same time which is what happened in a change from previous years. When they were published, the primary school figures revealed falling standards in reading, writing and mathematics among seven-year-olds and missed targets for 11-year-olds. The Code of Practice requires figures to be released as soon as available. It also became clear that ministers and their special advisers had substantial access to the statistics before they were released to the general public. The Statistics Commission told the department to stop special advisers having any influence on the publication of official figures.

In 2003, in his first political publication since retiring as an MP in 2001, the former Prime Minister John Major denounced Labour spin as *"the pornography of politics"* in a pamphlet published by the Centre for Policy Studies. He also said in an interview with the Daily Telegraph: *"Spin is the pornography of politics. It perverts. It is deceit licensed by the Government. Statistics massaged. Expenditure announced and reannounced. The record reassessed. Blame attributed. Innocence proclaimed. Black declared white: all in a day's work."*

It also turned out that there was surprising support from an unexpected source about the Blair Government's reputation for spinning its announcements. A leaked 2000 memo from Philip Gould, the Labour Party's market researcher and strategist, said that Blair was "*all show and no substance*". He referred to New Labour as a "*brand - rather like the latest soap powder - which has become badly contaminated*".

In 2004 the charity Migration Watch UK uncovered a series of papers which they described as casting a "*sinister light*" on the relationship between the Office for National Statistics ("ONS") and the Home Office. The ONS was shown to have asked the Home Office as to which method of reviewing the population projections would be most palatable to it from a presentational point of view, a question contrary to the ONS's responsibility for producing credible statistics.

Spin in Government statistics is difficult to deal with not only for the general public but also for the media. They will normally have deadlines to file a story and insufficient time to find alternative points of view to those portrayed by ministers. Statistics are always selective. As the Duke of Wellington said: *"Lies, damned lies and statistics"*.

A 2005 survey unsurprisingly demonstrated that 64% of people did not have confidence in the information presented by ministers on the basis of the data collected by the ONS. In the light of the various scandals which had taken place the Government had to accept that the ONS would become a Parliamentary agency outside any direct ministerial control.

2. <u>Establishment of the Statistics Authority</u>

A new UK Statistics Authority was proposed in 2006 which was billed by ministers as making the governance of national data independent of ministerial control for the first time. The new arrangements however have serious defects which were pointed out by its predecessor, the Statistics Commission, during the second reading of the Statistics and Registration Service Bill which set up the Authority.

The Statistics Commission said that it was concerned that the arrangements for the new Authority failed to take ministers out of the loop in the preparation and presentation of statistics. They stated that "*the Bill as presently drafted:*

- *does not secure a sufficiently clear separation of executive and scrutiny roles;:*
- *gives the Board responsibility for, but not authority over, official statistics in Government bodies other than ONS;*
- *does not place Government bodies under an explicit obligation to observe the Code of Practice;*
- *continues to let Ministers - rather than the Board on behalf of Parliament - determine the rules for access to statistics before they are published."*

The Shadow Chief Secretary, Theresa Villiers MP, similarly said in the Second Reading debate on the Bill in the House of Commons:

> *"Public trust in statistics is at an all time low. The Government had a golden opportunity to tackle this problem but its proposals simply do not go far enough. Conservatives would like to see public trust in official*

figures restored by taking politicians out of the process of production and release of Government statistics, and removing their power to manipulate and spin the figures for their own short term political ends."

"The Opposition will therefore be making great efforts to strengthen the bill during its passage through Parliament. We are tabling amendments in committee to ensure that the full rigour of the Government's reforms apply to all official statistics and not just those nominated by ministers to become National Statistics and to ensure there is a clear split between the people responsible for production of statistics and those who scrutinise them and the figures they produce. We also want to strengthen independence from ministers and radically restrict their pre-release access to statistics."

However there were no substantial changes to the Bill during its progress through Parliament to allay these concerns which still continue.

Although the new Statistics Authority has the theoretical responsibility for safeguarding the quality of all official statistics it does not have any commensurate authority over any statistics produced by Government departments. More than 80 per cent of all Government statisticians do not work for the ONS but for individual Government departments and similarly about four-fifths of all official statistics designated as 'National Statistics' are in fact produced by those individual departments. In addition responsibility for the production of statistics in Scotland, Wales and Northern Ireland lies with the devolved administrations for each nation in all areas for which they have devolved policy responsibility. This further clouds the production of UK figures.

Individual departments (or devolved nations) can consequently still produce whatever statistics they like with the only sanction being a possible retrospective comment by a Select Committee. The Code of Practice for National Statistics only focuses on statistical methods and the Commission stated that *"even full compliance will not buttress public confidence."* The Code is not even binding on all Government bodies. In addition the Authority still does not have the power to decide when ministers should have access to sensitive statistics when it is well known that such access has been used by ministers to spin the announcement of statistics in their direction rather than to give an honest view of the situation.

The establishment of the new UK Statistics Authority in 2008 seems to be a clear and cynical case of ministers having an opportunity to clean up a situation but deciding for party political reasons that they did not want to do so as this might well prejudice their ability to use the organs of Government for their own party political ends.

In launching the new UK Statistics Authority in April 2008 its independent chairman, former civil servant Sir Michael Scholar, agreed that people had minimal faith in official figures: *"We're starting against a very poor background of public trust. British statistics are held in high regard internationally but public confidence here is lower than in any other European (Union) country."* (The public level of trust was also possibly further blemished by media revelations that Sir Michael's son had coincidentally been appointed by Gordon Brown as his Chief of Staff at 10 Downing Street when he became Prime Minister.)

Sir Michael added at the launch of the Authority: *"From tomorrow, ministers are out of it. It should make a great difference to the level of public trust in statistics."* However although the new Authority will be answerable to Parliament this will be through a Select Committee on which the Government will, as usual, have its hand-picked majority. In addition none of the defects identified by the previous Statistics Commission and described above have been rectified and therefore the new Authority is essentially toothless in relation to the vast majority of Government statistics and their announcement.

Karen Dunnell, the National Statistician, explained what she saw as the meaning of independence for the ONS. She accepted that: *"We still have to abide by all the Civil Service rules. I can't stand up and say exactly what I like because that's not part of the Civil Service code".* She also identified a number of areas where the system still needed to be improved:

- Statisticians in Government departments rather than ministers should present their own statistics in press conferences whereas currently only the ONS does this.

- There should be a standard pre-release period during which ministers and other interested parties are given the statistics under embargo

As part of the new arrangements the Government also decided that the ONS in London should be reduced to fewer than 100 people and that the great bulk of its staff should be relocated to Newport or Titchfield. This was seen by many as undermining the new Statistics Authority by moving most of its people away from the departmental statisticians who still have London as their focus and generally as their base.

As expected by those who were critical of the proposals for the new Statistics Authority, the new arrangements have not significantly improved public confidence in Government statistics. In August 2008, Professor David Hand, head of the Royal Statistical Society, highlighted "*serious*" bad practices during the release of immigration figures in August. In December 2008 Sir Michael Scholar wrote formally to Jeremy Heywood, Permanent Secretary to the Prime Minister, to complain about the issuing by the Home Office of knife crime statistics whose release he described as "*premature, irregular and selective*". Sir Michael said in his letter that he had been told that officials or advisors in Number 10 had "*caused*" the Home Office to issue the release. The Office for National Statistics has also been concerned at how the Home Office has issued figures in other politically sensitive areas such as asylum and immigration.

3. <u>Recommended Action</u>

Other countries have faced a similar problem but have had the governance structures and political will to put in place a credible system for producing all Government statistics. For instance the Australian Bureau of Statistics (ABS) is responsible for producing statistics for all federal Government departments. If, for instance, an education or health department wishes to have a statistical review then it has to do this through the ABS.

This should be the model for the Statistics Authority in the UK in order to improve the credibility of Government measures. This would be a substantial dislocation with the departments losing their separate statisticians but there is no doubt that these people would be much more protected from political pressure if they were in a central ONS rather than depending for their careers on their superiors in their particular department.

Successive Governments have failed to act to provide the British people with a proper statistical service. The Jury Team believes that it is vital both to Government and to citizens that they have the most accurate and unbiased information available in order to make their decisions. It is therefore a priority of the Jury Team to sort out the provision of Government statistics, to ensure that they can never again be contaminated by party politics and therefore to establish a fully independent Statistics Authority directly responsible for all Government statistics. The members of the board of the Statistics Authority would be appointed by a panel nominated by seven relevant NGOs and other stakeholders who in this case might be The Royal Statistical Society, The Royal Economic Society, the Royal Society, The Market Research Society, The Strategic Planning Society, Universities UK and the Institute of Mathematics.

All Government statistics should be published by an independent body whose Board is appointed by a panel of designated NGOs and other stakeholders associated with the collection and use of statistics.

L. Enhancing Other Jurisdictions

a. European Union

1. UK Relationships with the European Union

Although there are differences in detail, the Jury Team Principles can also be applied to the institutions and organisation of the European Union and of local Government.

The relation of the UK to EU (formerly EEC) has been a central feature of UK politics for fifty years but its various enhancements have generally not received particularly strong parliamentary support:

- The Bill to join the EEC passed its Third Reading in the House of Commons in July 1972 by only 301 to 284 (16 Conservatives voted against and four abstained and there were 13 Labour abstentions).

- For the Single European Act 1986 there was a Government three-line Whip and a 'guillotine'.

- At Second Reading on the Maastricht Treaty, the European Communities (Amendment) Bill, in May 1992, 22 Conservative MPs defied the Whip and voted against.

- For the Treaty of Amsterdam in late 1997 there was an Opposition three-line whip and only one MP, Edward Heath, defied the party whip by abstaining.

- For the vote on the Treaty of Nice in 2004 there was an Opposition and a Government three-line whip and the Government won with a large majority even though 100 Labour MPs did not even attend.

2. Referendums on the EU

The parties have taken varying positions on having a referendum on Europe. Enoch Powell and Neil Marten put down an amendment calling for a referendum on entry to the EEC in 1972. This was pursued in March 1972 by Tony Benn who took it to the National Executive where it became official Labour policy in April 1972. Labour in opposition also voted in favour of a referendum on the Maastricht Treaty but in Government they were against referendums on the Amsterdam and Nice Treaties.

The Conservative leadership were against a referendum on UK membership of the EEC in 1972 and also against a referendum on the Single European Act and Maastricht Treaties although in the Maastricht vote in April 1993, 72 Conservatives voted for a referendum. In June 1997 the Leader of the Conservatives, William Hague, made a call for a referendum on the Amsterdam Treaty at the Scottish Conservative Conference but had reversed his position by October when the matter was debated in the Commons.

The Liberal Democrats were divided over a referendum on Maastricht in 1993 when twelve of their MPs supported a referendum while four were against. They were against referendums on the Amsterdam and Nice Treaties.

Under pressure before the European Parliament election in 2004 Tony Blair suddenly promised a referendum on the new EU Constitution, which was supported by the Conservatives and Liberal Democrats, but he then decided against a referendum on its somewhat modified version the Lisbon Treaty. Voters did not take kindly to such a change in commitment and a poll found 83% of Britons favoured a referendum, especially as some other EU countries intended to put the constitution before their voters.

The Conservatives have since called for a referendum on the Lisbon Treaty and have said that they will hold one if they return to power before the Treaty is ratified by all the other countries and have hinted that they might do so even if it has been ratified. The Liberal Democrats have been split again over the Lisbon Treaty.

It is however very clear that people across Europe wanted to have a referendum on the new EU Constitution/Lisbon Treaty. A 2007 poll published by the think-tank Open Europe across all 27 countries showed the following response to the question: *"If a new treaty is drawn up which gives more powers to the EU do you think that people should be given a say on this in a referendum or citizen consultation or do you think that it should just be up to the national Parliament to ratify this treaty?"*. An average of 75% were in favour of having a referendum, with 83% in the UK:

	Yes to referendum	No to Referendum	Don't Know
Ireland	87%	11%	1%
Greece	83%	14%	3%
UK	**83%**	15%	3%
Czech Republic	82%	15%	3%
France	81%	16%	3%
Latvia	80%	11%	10%
Malta	77%	17%	6%
Germany	77%	23%	1%
Cyprus	76%	21%	3%
Estonia	74%	16%	11%
Poland	74%	16%	10%

Luxemburg	74%	23%	3%
Denmark	73%	22%	4%
Spain	73%	24%	3%
Belgium	73%	25%	2%
Finland	72%	25%	3%
Bulgaria	71%	13%	16%
Austria	71%	25%	4%
Italy	70%	23%	8%
Sweden	68%	30%	2%
Lithuania	67%	15%	18%
Romania	66%	11%	23%
Hungary	66%	30%	4%
Slovakia	64%	20%	16%
Portugal	64%	21%	15%
Netherlands	62%	29%	9%
Slovenia	55%	40%	4%
Total	**75%**	20%	5%

Another example of ambivalence was David Cameron's statement in December 2005 that he wanted to withdraw the Conservative MEPs from the European People's Party - European Democrats group of the European Parliament. Kenneth Clarke described this as a "*head-banging*" policy. A majority of Tory MEPs also oppose David Cameron's stance. In February 2006 The Times reported: *"The Tory leader has been told that senior figures such as Angela Merkel, the German Chancellor, and Silvio Berlusconi, the Italian Prime Minister, are threatening to cut bilateral relations. In all 11 leaders of right-wing governments and parties have said that they will refuse to work with Mr Cameron if he withdraws Tory MEPs from the European People's Party grouping in the European Parliament. The list includes Nicolas Sarkozy, the French Interior Minister and likely presidential candidate, and Mariano Rasjoy, the head of the opposition Spanish Popular Party."*

3. The Effect of the UK's Unclear Relationship with the EU

The UK's party political prevarication on the EU over forty years has weakened our dealings with continental Europe. Countries such as Switzerland and Norway that have stayed outside the EU have prospered. Similarly others such as Ireland and Portugal which have embraced it have also done well.

The constant policy turns by the UK have however meant that neither have our best people sought election to the European Parliament nor has our Government machine given it a high priority by ensuring that our most able officials are seconded to Brussels and given every help in securing senior positions in the EU management structures. Our last four appointments as a UK Commissioner have been:

- Neil Kinnock: former Labour Party leader appointed in 1995 who had to resign with the rest of the Commission over fraud charges in 1999, returning to serve until 2004

- Chris Patten: Former MP and Chairman of the Conservative Party who lost his seat in 1992 and served in Brussels from 2000 to 2004. Nominated for the post of President in the new Commission in 2004 but unable to gain support from France and Germany

- Peter Mandelson: MP forced twice to resign from Tony Blair's Cabinet. Given the consolation prize of European Commissioner by Tony Blair. Served from 2004 to 2008 when he was unexpectedly brought back by Gordon Brown for a third term as a Cabinet minister and given a peerage

- Baroness Ashton: previously a charity worker before getting her life peerage, she entered Cabinet in 2007 as Leader of the House of Lords. Appointed to replace Mandelson in 2008 as Trade Commissioner for party political reasons to prevent a by-election if a Labour MP had been appointed.

The ambivalence of the UK's relationship with the EU has also meant that business and NGOs have not built up as strong links with the EU as have other countries which tend to have far more active lobbying groups in Brussels.

This ambivalence is only likely to stop if there is a UK referendum on continuing EU membership, something which the Jury Team expects would result from its governance proposals on referendums and which is supported by several political parties and by a wide share of the population.

4. EU Governance

The EU has many key governance issues and fails ordinary tests for both transparency and accountability. At the highest level the European Court of Auditors has qualified the accounts of the European Community for each of the last 14 years. The report for the year 2006 included the following comments:

- Accounting system: "*The Court's audit has identified errors in amounts registered in the accounting system as invoices/cost statements and pre-financing which have the effect of overstating the accounts payable by some 201 million euros and the total amount of long and short term pre-financing by some 656 million euros.*" (p.14).

- CAP: The Court notices improvements in some areas, but "*structural measures and internal policies show that complicated rules or unclear eligibility criteria or complex legal requirements have a considerable impact on the legality and regularity of the underlying transactions. In these areas, which cover a significant part of the budget, checks on expenditure claims, which are mainly based on the information supplied by the beneficiary are, in many cases, insufficient in number and coverage and often of inadequate quality.*" (p.10).

- Single Payment Scheme: 28.9% of payments checked contained errors (p.99). "*For 2006 the Court has confirmed continuing failure to implement key controls, namely: claims handling, inspection procedures, animal database integrity and the Land Parcel Identification System. Some 850 million euro per year is paid to farmers under these unsatisfactory control conditions.*" (p.100)

- External Aid: In 9 of 11 projects audited, on the spot, procedures were not followed (p.185). In 3, money was spent ineligibly; in 4, receipts were not kept.

- Committee of the Regions: "*In various cases, travel expenditure was refunded on the basis of hand-written travel agency invoices always showing the same amount. In the context of an ex post verification procedure the Committee's administration found that this amount was on average 83%*

higher than the price charged by the airline for the ticket used."

- MEPs' Administrative Expenditure: MEP allowances in 2006 ran to €132 million (p. 217). MEPs were supposed to start showing receipts in 2005. The deadline has been adjusted by the MEPs several times (with receipts still having to be shown supposedly from 2005!). *"As the major part of the amounts paid for MEPs assistance allowance have not been subsequently justified by appropriate supporting documents of the expenses incurred on behalf of the MEPs, the Court considers that there is not sufficient documentation to demonstrate that the MEPs have actually employed or engaged the services of one or more assistants and that the duties or services mentioned in the contracts signed by the MEPs have been really carried out."*

In his book appropriately entitled *"The Gravy Train"*, Philip Bushill-Matthews, currently the leader of the Conservative MEPs (having taken over from Giles Chichester MEP who resigned following an expenses scandal), identified a number of specific administrative failures in detail of which four are summarised here:

- The Case of the Flaming Flax: High subsidies to Spanish flax farmers to produce flax which was known to be unmarketable and then *"accidentally"* destroyed

- The Case of the Irish-Polish Butter: Food aid butter to Russia diverted to Poland by a French company that was fined €17.6 million but had its fine cut by 80% by the Cabinet of the French EU President Jacques Delors whose office had lost the minutes of the relevant meeting when challenged by the Court of Auditors. The police eventually arrested 30 people but a number of the senior Commission officials involved continued to occupy their positions

- The Case of the ECHO Submarines: ECHO is the European Communities Humanitarian Office and between 1993 and 1995 up to €550 million could not be accounted for. Submarines are people unofficially employed. Money was sent to an EU-funded office in Sarajevo which turned out not to exist. The Commission admitted that 2,000 documents had been destroyed. By 2000, internal audit revealed that over €1 billion had been paid without any receipts.

- <u>The Case of the Emerging Entrepreneurs</u>: The European Development Fund sent €73 million to the Ivory Coast to boost entrepreneurship. After the programme was finished it emerged that at least a third of the money had been embezzled. The Commission failed to identify one enterprising group which operated six different identities with just one address, telephone and fax number.

5. <u>MEPs' Remuneration and Expenses</u>

British MEPs receive £63,291 a year, the same as Westminster MPs. However after July 2009 their pay after tax could rise from about £46,835 to almost £69,000 a year, depending on the exchange rate and whether they will be allowed to pay the lower European Union tax rate of 15%.

The issue of MEPs' expenses is a particularly serious one in the eyes of voters. MEPs can claim up to £160,054 annually for staff, £38,340 for office costs and £82,490 for subsistence and accommodation and there are also very generous travel allowances. There is no detailed auditing of how the money is spent

In November 2008 an inquiry by the European Parliament found Dan Dover, a British Conservative MEP, guilty of a conflict of interest, and he was ordered to repay £500,000 of expenses that he had paid to his wife and daughter for over nine years. This followed the resignation of the Conservatives' Leader in Europe, Giles Chichester, who resigned because he paid for secretarial and office work through a company of which he was a director.

Despite the criticism by the Court of Auditors quoted above, a more detailed report, which did not name any MEPs anyway, was not published and could only be viewed in a special secure room. In March 2008 the campaigning anti-corruption MEP Paul Van Buitenen broke the Parliament's secrecy rules and published a short summary of the report on his website. The report noted MEPs who were paying funds into their own companies and one MEP who was claiming £130,000 for staff while not employing anyone.

However, in April 2008 MEPs still voted against publishing the report. Chris Davies, a Liberal Democrat MEP, commented that *"Far from cleaning up their act, a majority of MEPs seem intent on allowing greed and self-interest to triumph over the proper financial management of public money".*

In February 2009 Jonathan Oliver reported in The Sunday Times the details of the report:

"A leaked internal report has revealed systematic abuses by Euro MPs of parliamentary allowances that enable them to pocket more than £1m in profits from a single five-year term. The auditor's confidential report, suppressed by the Brussels parliament, discloses the extraordinary frauds used by MEPs to siphon off staff allowances funded by taxpayers. It shows that some claimed for paying assistants of whom no record exists, awarded them bonuses of up to 1½ times annual salary and diverted public money into front companies. A copy of the 92-page report, prepared by Robert Galvin, the parliament's head of internal audit, has been seen by The Sunday Times. It reveals:

> *- Payments were made to assistants who were not accredited with the European parliament and to companies whose accounts showed no activity.*
>
> *- End-of-year bonuses worth up to 19½ times monthly salary were paid to assistants to allow members to use up their full annual allowance.*
>
> *- Payments, supposedly for secretarial work, were made to a crèche whose manager happened to be a local politician from the MEP's political party.*
>
> *- One MEP claimed to have paid the full £182,000 staff allowance to one person, suspected of being a relative.*

MEPs also have a final salary pension scheme which is even more generous than the one provided to members of the Westminster parliament. The TaxPayers' Alliance calculates that the cash value of this benefit would be about £350,000 over a full parliamentary term.

At current exchange rates the grand total profit over five years comes to £1,176,800. That figure does not include an MEP's salary."

Peter Mandelson's salary payments and pension arrangements from being an EU Commissioner for just four years and voluntarily resigning have also shone a light on the excesses of EU remuneration. Mandelson receives a monthly 'transition allowance' to maintain his salary for three years at the level he enjoyed in Brussels (a top up of £78,000 p.a. - based on the difference between his previous £182,500 salary in Brussels and his new salary as a UK minister). The cash cushion will be taxed at only 26 per cent under special 'community rates' open to EU officials. When he reaches the age of 65, Mandelson will receive an inflation adjusted pension, starting at £31,000, despite only four years in the job, and then rising in line with the cost of living, valued in the private sector as requiring a fund of around £750,000. As he relocates from Brussels to London, Mandelson is also due a one-off resettlement grant of some £15,000.

6. Voters' Views of the EU

The European Union therefore exhibits many of the characteristics which have led to the formation of the Jury Team. It seems to many to be unaccountable, distant, and staffed by people who are more worried about their own careers than the public benefit, with all of this being overlaid by a perception that its MEPs and officials are on an expenses *"gravy train"* and that the whole edifice is infiltrated by fraud.

The latest Eurobarometer survey in May 2008 by the European Commission itself confirmed the low esteem in which the EU is held by its citizens, not just those in the UK. Only 48% of all EU citizens across the 27 countries agreed with the statement that: *"Does the European Union conjure up for you a positive image?"*. A very low 29% of UK citizens agreed with the statement and 34% had a negative image.

In the same report the Commission states: *"Positive views on Membership of the EU are on (sic) decline"* and *"Fewer Europeans now say that their country's membership is a good thing compared to autumn 2007"*. It also reports: *"In this wave we find that the majority view in the UK has turned negative with 32% of respondents saying that their country's membership is a bad thing, against 30% who say either that it is a good thing or who cannot form an opinion in this respect."*

Similarly in the same survey when asked: *"Taking everything into account, would you say that the UK has on balance benefited or not from being a member of the European Union?"* 50% said it had not benefited and only 36% said it had benefited.

This Eurobarometer survey also asked: *"I would like to ask you a question about how much trust you have in certain institutions. For each of the following institutions, please tell me if you tend to trust it or tend not to trust it."* It has already been noted above in Chapter 1 that in line with the thesis of the Jury Team, only 27% of UK citizens said they trusted the UK Parliament and only 24% said they trusted the UK Government. However UK citizens at 29% also had the lowest trust in the EU of any of the 27 countries:

<u>Tend to trust the European Union</u>

Cyprus	71%	Czech Republic	59%
Estonia	69%	Poland	59%
Belgium	68%	Greece	59%
Slovakia	67%	Portugal	58%
Spain	66%	Luxembourg	55%
Slovenia	66%	Finland	52%
Romania	66%	Hungary	52%
Malta	65%	France	50%
Bulgaria	63%	Sweden	47%
Ireland	62%	Latvia	46%
Lithuania	62%	Germany	43%
Denmark	60%	Italy	40%
Netherlands	59%	Austria	38%
		UK	**29%**

In response to similar specific questions about trust in the European Parliament and in the European Commission, the UK again had the lowest scores of any of the 27 countries with just

27% trusting the European Parliament and 24% trusting the European Commission.

In October 2007 the European Commission asked citizens across the EU how well informed they felt about the European Parliament. 81% in the UK said they were "Badly informed" and only 18% said "Well informed" (1% were Don't Know). When asked the timing of the next European Parliamentary election, only 2% of the respondents correctly said 2009, 4% said other years and a huge 94% told the Commission's researchers that they did not know.

7. The Issues in the European Elections

In April 2008 the Commission asked 27,000 citizens across Europe, including 1,300 in the UK, about what issues would be important to them in the next European elections. The top six responses were:

Immigration	49%
Terrorism	46%
Crime	43%
Economic Growth	31%
Unemployment	29%
Climate Change	29%

None of these are obviously party political issues on which either Labour, Conservatives or Liberal Democrats have a winning position.

When asked what they would look for in a candidate, the top four responses were:

Experience in European affairs	35%
Position on national issues	31%
Experience of candidate at national level	29%
Position on European issues	28%

It is again notable that none of these criteria are party political but seek candidates with real experience.

8. The 2009 European Election

The results of the 2004 European elections were:

	Votes	%	Seats	%
Conservative Party	4,397,090	25.9%	27	34.6%
Labour Party	3,718,683	21.9%	19	24.4%
UK Ind. Party	2,660,768	15.6%	12	15.4%
Liberal Democrats	2,452,327	14.4%	12	15.4%
Green Party	1,028,283	6.0%	2	2.6%
Scottish National Party	231,505	1.4%	2	2.6%
DUP	175,761	1.0%	1	1.3%
Plaid Cymru	159,888	0.9%	1	1.3%
Sinn Féin	144,541	0.8%	1	1.3%
UUP	91,164	0.5%	1	1.3%
Other Parties	1,947,693	11.5%	0	0.0%
Total valid votes	17,007,703	100.0%	78	100.0%

Spoiled / rejected	138,856
VOTES CAST	17,146,559
Electorate	44,157,400
TURN OUT	38.8%

Over three fifths of the electorate did not vote. Labour and the Conservatives together only achieved 47.8% of the actual vote or just 18.4% of those entitled to vote. In relation to their number of votes, the Conservatives did better in terms of seats as their support was concentrated in the South, South West and Eastern regions. The Scottish, Welsh and Northern Ireland parties also achieved a higher percentage of seats than votes because of their geographical concentration. However the 1.9 million votes cast for "Other Parties" gained no seats and the Greens, being geographically spread, also received less than half of their vote percentage in terms of seats.

The Daily Telegraph reported the results of a January 2009 YouGov poll as follows:

"In the first study of voting intentions for the European parliamentary elections in June the Tories are on 35 per cent, six points ahead of Labour on 29 per cent with the Liberal Democrats on 15 per cent and UKIP on 7 per cent. Then come the Greens (5 per cent), the British National Party (4 per cent) and nationalist parties in Scotland and Wales (also 4 per cent).

Significantly, 10 per cent of Conservative voters at a general election would switch to UKIP in the euro-election, compared with 2 per cent of Labour voters and 1 per cent of those backing the Lib Dems. Conservative support could fall still further if Mr Clarke makes a front-bench return, using his position to make high-profile interventions on European matters."

In the same report The Daily Telegraph also stated:

"Overall, 16 per cent of voters want Britain simply to withdraw from the EU, while 48 per cent would like to see a much looser relationship, with the government taking back powers from Brussels and ending the supremacy of the European Court of Justice over British law.

Added together this makes 64 per cent in favour of weakening Britain's ties with the EU, compared with just 22 per cent in favour of keeping the UK's current full membership including the Lisbon Treaty, which was passed by parliament without a referendum.

Some 45 per cent of voters, meanwhile, believe none of the three main political parties adequately reflects their views on Britain's future relations with the EU."

The 2009 European Parliament election is therefore wide open. Many who voted Conservative and Labour are likely to support the Jury Team's proposals to take a strong line on corruption and sleaze in the EU. Many of those supporting either UKIP or the Liberal Democrats will see the opportunity of a referendum on the EU through support for the Jury Team as a way of establishing once and for all whether or not the UK should stay in the EU.

b. Local and Devolved Government

1. Voters' Views of Local Government

As well as the European Union, the other main legislative groupings that affect citizens are local and devolved government, including the Scottish Parliament and the Welsh and Northern Ireland Assemblies.

Citizen engagement with local government is very weak. Ipsos/MORI conducted a survey of just over a thousand adults in Greater London in April 2008. This showed that although just under two-thirds of Londoners think they know which political party is in control of the Council, in practice fewer than half actually do. In answer to the question *"Do you know which political party is in control of your local London Borough council?"* 63% said yes and 35% said no. However when the 63% were asked *"Can you tell me which party is in control of your local London Borough council?"*, only 66% of those who had claimed to know actually chose the right party. This means that only 66% of 63%, i.e. 42%, of the total electorate actually know which party runs their local council

The position was even worse when these London voters were asked *"Do you know the name of the local elected leader of your local London Borough council?"* Only one in five claimed to know and of these only one third got the right answer to the question *"Can you tell me the name of the person who is local elected leader of your local London Borough council?"* this means that only 33% of 20% or less than one in 14 Londoners actually know the name of their local council leader.

Unfortunately the general public also does not have a good image of local councillors. In a study by Ipsos/MORI in conjunction with the Standards Board for England in July 2005, people across England were asked about the motives of councillors. In answer to the question *"In general, whose interests do you think councillors put first?"* the response showed that a massive 68% of the public think they put first their own interest, the party's interest or their friends' and family's interest. Only 25% of the public think that councillors put first the interests of their local area:

Their own	32%
Their party's	27%
Their friends' and family's	9%
Total Non-civic	**68%**
The local area's interests	25%
Don't know	8 %
Total	**100%**

2. <u>Independent Councillors</u>

In the London survey it is however interesting to note that when asked *"Does your Council promote the interests of local residents?"* the percentage agreeing "a great deal" or "to some extent" was highest at 70% in the City of London which, as mentioned in Chapter 2 above, does not have any political parties. The average for all of the 33 councils of London was 16 points lower at only 54% with the lowest being Havering at 45%.

For well over 100 years there have been Independent councillors serving their communities. Across the UK there are now more than 2,000 Independent Councillors (those not belonging to a national or devolved nation party). Independent councillors give the electorate more choice, help to unlock voter apathy and are not diverted by national political party agendas.

The local Government elections in 2007 and 2008 also show the validity of the Jury Team model. Of the 310 councils who had members up in England for election in the 2007 local elections, over a quarter, 85, resulted in a hung council with no overall control and therefore either an independent, minority or party compromise administration.

In the May 2007 local Government elections there was a particular example of success by a group of Independents in Boston, Lincolnshire. The headline on the day after the election said: "*Boston Council driven into the Sea by Transport Protestors*". 25 of the 32 seats on Boston Council were won by the Boston Bypass Independents Group who were not from a Green party objecting to development but rather demanding that the council "*get its act together*" to decide on a transport system to sort out congestion in the town. This Independent group achieved more than half of the total votes cast which led to their winning 25 of the 32 seats, removing all of the Labour and Liberal Democrat councillors and more than halving the number of Tories from twelve to five. Richard Austin, leader of the newly elected group, said the victory came as no surprise: "*We knew that the mood of the people of Boston was very black and they really do want something to happen to Boston that isn't happening at the moment.*"

In May 2007 there were also local Government elections in Scotland for all 32 unitary authority councils. The results showed the importance of Independent councillors. Only 2 councils had a party winning a majority of seats, those being Glasgow and North Lanarkshire with Labour majorities of 58% and 57% of the councillors.

All of the 30 other councils had either Independent councillors running them, coalitions or minority administrations. The outcome included 12 of the councils having Independents in their administration:

- 3: Run by Independents with Orkney and Shetland having no political party councillors and 100% Independent councillors and Comhairle Nan Eilean Siar having 81% Independent councillors.

- 3: Independents are the largest grouping in Moray, Highland and Argyll & Bute with 46%, 43% and 42% of the seats respectively and govern in conjunction with the Conservatives in Moray and with the SNP in the other two councils

- 6: Independents also form part of the governing administration in Angus, West Dunbartonshire, Falkirk, West Lothian, East Renfrewshire and Scottish Borders.

In the remaining 18 there is a complete mixture of administrations:

- Majority coalition:
    - 6: Liberal Democrat and SNP majority
    - 1: in Aberdeenshire a Conservative-Liberal Democrat majority
    - 1: in the City of Dundee a Labour-Liberal Democrat majority

- Minority administration:
  - 8: one party minority: Labour (5), SNP (2) and Conservative (1)
  - 1: in East Dunbartonshire a Conservative-Labour minority
  - 1: in Dumfries & Galloway a Conservative-Liberal Democrat minority

In May 2008 there were local Government elections in Wales and in certain parts of England. The Welsh elections saw a substantial increase in the number of Independent members with them becoming part of the administration in 16 out of the 22 councils in Wales. As well as having overall control in Powys and Pembrokeshire, the Independents also lead administrations in seven other councils, Blaenau Gwent, Carmarthenshire, Ceredigion, Flintshire, Merthyr, Anglesey and Denbighshire. They are junior partners on a further seven councils. Independent Councillor John Davies, Pembrokeshire, is now the head of the Welsh Local Government Association (WLGA) with the Independents having swept away the former Labour domination of this group.

Fran Yeoman described the success of the Welsh Independent candidates in a May 2008 article in The Times entitled *"Independents charge through the Valleys and seize the reins"*:

"Newport, the last Welsh city in the Labour party's hands after 2004, fell to no overall control, and Flintshire, the only authority it had held in the North, went the same way. But it was in the valleys that Labour's bedrock of support most dramatically collapsed. Independents delivered the knockout blows as former Labour supporters in the region gave their backing to local groups and individual candidates.

Labour councils in Merthyr Tydfil, Blaenau Gwent, Torfaen and Caerphilly were all toppled. In the first two of these, independents and local parties had the numbers to take overall control, while in Torfaen independents became the second largest group, just two behind Labour's eighteen seats.

Mr Morgan {Rhodri Morgan, the Labour leader and First Minister} spoke darkly of an 'anti-politician mood', claiming that 'protest candidates are doing very well' after 'a huge amount of bad news about the economy'."

In the elections in England in May 2008, there were 129 councils with their seats being contested. Again the situation of no overall control increased with there being 46 councils, 36%, in this position including Birmingham, Blackburn, Bolton, Bradford, Carlisle, Cheltenham, Colchester, Coventry, Derby, Doncaster, Exeter, Gloucester, Harrogate, Hartlepool, Hastings, Ipswich, Leeds, Liverpool, Milton Keynes, Northumberland, Norwich, Oxford, Portsmouth, Preston, Reading, Warrington, Weymouth, Wolverhampton and Worcester. In addition there were 12 councils under the control of the Liberal Democrats, 15 under Labour and 56 under the Conservatives, mainly in rural seats.

3. <u>2009/10/11 Local Government Elections</u>

The Jury Team has considered whether to run in the local Government elections in 2009 but in fact there are none scheduled in either Scotland or Wales. In England there are only local Government elections in 34 councils (compared with the 129 in 2008) which are predominantly county councils in central and southern England (there are also four mayoral elections anticipated in Doncaster, Hartlepool, North Tyneside and Stoke).

The Jury Team therefore considers that in 2009 it is better to focus its efforts on the European elections which will be held on the same day as the local government elections in England, 4th June 2009, and similarly in 2010 the main emphasis is likely to be on the general election.

The Jury Team does however expect to be able to contribute fully to the local elections in 2011 which are the main ones of the four year cycle of such elections.

4. 2007 and 2011 Devolved Nation Elections

SCOTLAND 2007	Votes		Seats	
SNP	1,297,838	33.2%	47	36.4%
Labour	1,243,789	31.8%	46	35.7%
Conservative	618,778	15.8%	17	13.2%
Lib Dem	556,883	14.3%	16	12.4%
Green	85,548	2.2%	2	1.6%
Other Parties	85,457	2.2%	0	0.0%
Margo Macdonald	19,256	0.5%	1	0.8%
	3,907,549	100.0%	129	100.00%
Turnout	51.7%			

WALES 2007	Votes		Seats	
Labour	603,879	30.9%	26	43.3%
Conservative	427,883	21.9%	12	20.0%
Plaid Cymru	423,878	21.7%	15	25.0%
Lib Dem	258,950	13.3%	6	10.0%
People's Voice	16,070	0.8%	1	1.7%
Other Parties	222,356	11.3%	0	0.0%
	1,953,016	100.0%	60	100.0%
Turnout	43.3%			

N. IRELAND 2007	FP Votes		Seats	
DUP	207,721	30.1%	36	33.3%
Sinn Fein	180,573	26.2%	28	25.9%
SDLP	105,164	15.2%	16	14.8%
UUP	103,145	14.9%	18	16.7%
Alliance	36,139	5.2%	7	6.5%
Independent	31,312	4.5%	1	0.9%
PUP	3,822	0.6%	1	0.9%
Other Parties	22,437	3.3%	0	0.0%
Total	690,313	100.0%	108	100.0%
Turnout	62.3%			

The next elections for the Welsh Assembly and the Scottish Parliament are in May 2011. This is the same time as the next elections for the Assembly in Northern Ireland where there will also simultaneously be the elections for the 11 new District Councils, which will replace the current 26, whose elections are being deferred from 2009. The Jury Team expects to be in a strong position to field candidates in all of these 2011 elections in Wales, Scotland and Northern Ireland as well as in the local elections in England.

Appendix 1

Recommended Reading

Author	Title	Publisher
Introduction		
Peter Oborne	The Rise of the Political Class	Pocket Books
Patrick Dunleavy et al.	Developments in British Politics	Palgrave Macmillan
Andrew Marr	A History of Modern Britain	Pan Books
Anthony Sampson	Who Runs This Place?	John Murray
Patrick Dunleavy et al.	Voices of the People	Politico's
Political Parties		
Darren G. Lilleker	The Marketing of Political Parties	Manchester
Alan Ware	Political Parties and Party Systems	Oxford
Robert Garner and Richard Kelly	British Political Parties Today	Manchester
Parliament		
Michael Rush	Parliament Today	Manchester
Graham Allen MP	The Last Prime Minister	Imprint Academic
Ed. Keith Sutherland	The Rape of the Constitution	Imprint Academic
David Beetham et al	Democracy under Blair	Politico's

David Butler and Gareth Butler	British Political Facts Since 1979	Palgrave Macmillan
Peter Oborne	The Rise of Political Lying	Simon & Schuster

<u>Government</u>

Peter Hennessy	Whitehall	Fontana Press
Sir Christopher Foster	British Government in Crisis	Hart Publishing

<u>Elections</u>

David Denver	Elections and Voters in Britain	Palgrave Macmillan
Dennis Kavanagh and David Butler	The British General Election of 2005	Palgrave Macmillan
John Bartle, Anthony King	Britain at the Polls 2005	CQ Press

<u>Europe</u>

Michaela Maier, Jens Tenscher	Campaigning in Europe - Campaigning for Europe	Transaction Publishers
Philip Bushill-Matthews	The Gravy Train	Polperro Heritage

<u>Referendums</u>

Matt Qvortrup	A Comparative Study of Referendums	Manchester
James Willliam Sullivan	Direct Legislation by the Citizenship	BiblioBazaar
David Butler and Austin Ranney	Referendums Around the World	AEI

Independents

James Surowiecki	The Wisdom of Crowds	Random House
Richard Berry	Independent: The Rise of the Non-Aligned Politician	Imprint Academic
Keith Sutherland	A People's Parliament	Imprint Academic

Websites

Backbench Behaviour	www.revolts.co.uk
Be a Councillor	www.beacouncillor.org.uk
Civitas	www.civitas.org.uk
ConservativeHome	www.conservativehome.blogs.com
Convention on Modern Liberty	www.modernliberty.net
Democratic Audit	www.democraticaudit.com
Electoral Reform Society	www.electoral-reform.org.uk
E-Politix	www.epolitix.com
European Parliament	www.europarl.europa.eu
Fixed Term Parliaments	www.fixedterm.org.uk
Freedom of Information	www.cfoi.org.uk
Hansard Society	www.hansard-society.org.uk
House of Commons	www.parliament.uk/commons
Ian Dale's Diary	www.iaindale.blogspot.com
Independents' Network	www.independentnetwork.org.uk
Keele University Sources	www.psr.keele.ac.uk/area/uk.htm
Labour Union Digest	www.labouruniondigest.org.uk
MySociety	www.mysociety.org
Number 10 Petitions	www.petitions.number10.gov.uk
Open Democracy	www.opendemocracy.net
Political Analysis	www.politicalbetting.com
Public Whip	www.publicwhip.org.uk
Taxpayers' Alliance	www.taxpayersalliance.com
They Work For You	www.theyworkforyou.com
Unlock Democracy	www.unlockdemocracy.org.uk

Appendix2

Application to become a

Jury Team Candidate as a

Member of the Westminster Parliament

In which Region Would You Like to be a Candidate?

East Midlands

In which Constituency Would You Like to be a Candidate?

Amber Valley

Items shown with an Asterisk* will not be displayed for public view

Please Provide The Following Information

Your Name

Name by which you wish to be known:

Title: First Name:

Middle Names:

Surname:

Jury Team Candidate Name:

Gender: Male

Female

Short Description of Yourself as a Candidate (80 Characters)

Photo:

Home Address

First Line*:

Second Line*:

Third Line*:

City/Town:

County:

Postcode:

Contact Details

Home telephone number*:

Daytime telephone number*:

Email Address: [ ]

Date of Birth (dd/mm/yyyy)

Day*: [ ] Month*: [ ] Year: [ ]

Country of Birth

United Kingdom ▾

Nationality (if you have more than one nationality, indicate the first one in order which applies to you):

- (•) United Kingdom
- ( ) Irish Republic
- ( ) Commonwealth Country: [ ]
- ( ) Other EU: NOT VALID AS A WESTMINSTER CANDIDATE
- ( ) Other Country: NOT VALID AS A WESTMINSTER CANDIDATE

Have You Been A Member of Any Political Party at any time since the end of 2003?

- ( ) No
- ( ) Yes Which Political Party?

[ ]

Please Provide a Summary of Your Life and Career (Maximum 1,500 Characters)

Please Describe Why You Would Like To Represent This Constituency in the Westminster Parliament and any Local Issues on which you would Campaign (Maximum 500 Characters)

Please Describe Your Current Paid And Voluntary Roles (Up to Seven)

1.
2.
3.
4.
5.
6.
7.

Please Describe Your Previous Paid and Voluntary Roles (Starting With The Earliest)

1. Years:

2. Years:

3. Years:

4. Years:

5. Years:

6. Years:

7. Years:

Please Describe Your Education (Starting With The Earliest)

1. Years: School/College Name and Location

Achievements:

2. Years: School/College Name and Location

Achievements:

3. Years: School/College Name and Location

Achievements:

4. Years: School/College Name and Location

Achievements:

5. Years: School/College Name and Location

Achievements:

6. Years: School/College Name and Location

Achievements:

7. Years: School/College Name and Location

Achievements:

What Languages Other Than English Do You Speak?

Fluently:

Reasonably:

Slightly:

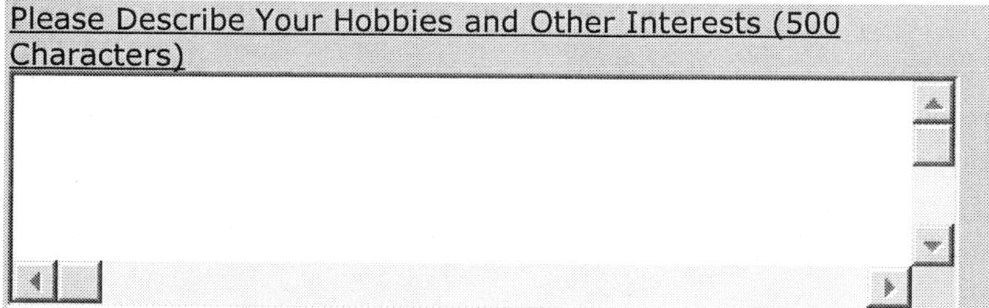
Please Describe Your Hobbies and Other Interests (500 Characters)

In Up To Three of These Areas, Please Describe Your Reason for Your Interest in Them and Your Own Views of the Main Policies That You Would Support

Agriculture and Food
Borders and Migration
Business, Management and Enterprise
Charities, Communities and Equalities
Culture, Heritage, Tourism, Marketing and Media
Defence
Energy
Environment and Nature
European and Foreign Affairs
Finance, Trade and Economics
Health, Social Care and Families
Housing and Planning
International Development
Justice, Crime and Security
Local Government
Parenting, Youth, Education and Skills
Pensions and Retirement
Science and Engineering
Sport, Adventure and Exploration
Taxation and Social Security
Transport

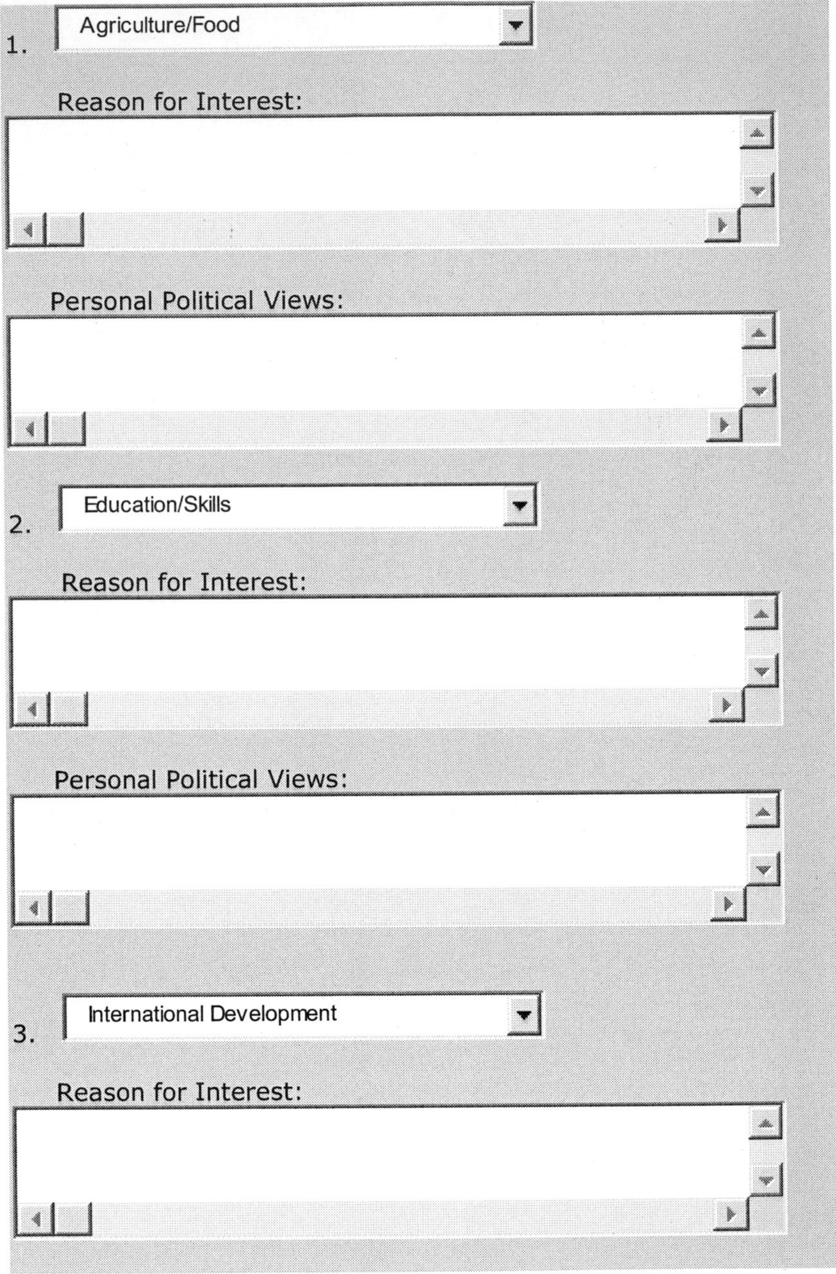
1. Agriculture/Food

Reason for Interest:

Personal Political Views:

2. Education/Skills

Reason for Interest:

Personal Political Views:

3. International Development

Reason for Interest:

Personal Political Views:

Please Give Your Views On Any Other Political Issues Which Are Important To You, Ensuring That You Mention Any Issue On Which You Will Be Campaigning (500 Characters)

Please Add Any Other Information That You Would Like To Provide (5,000 characters)

Password

Provide a Password so that you can access this form to make changes (minimum 6 characters)*:

Retype the Password to confirm it*:

The Following Two People In My Chosen Constituency Propose and Second My Nomination

PROPOSER

Name

Name by which they are known:

Surname: First Name:

Middle Names:

Home Address

First Line*:

Second Line*:

Third Line*:

City/Town:

County:

Postcode:

Contact Details

Home telephone number*:

Daytime telephone number*:

Email address:

Date of Birth

Day*: Month*: Year:

A Summary of My Proposer's Life and Career

His/Her Reason For Supporting Me (In Their Words)

SECONDER

Name

Name by which they are known:

Surname: First Name:

Middle Names:

Home Address

First Line*:

Second Line*:

Third Line*:

City/Town:

County:

Postcode:

Contact Details

Home telephone number*:

Daytime telephone number*:

Email address:

Date of Birth

Day*: Month*: Year:

A Summary of My Seconder's Life and Career

His/Her Reason For Supporting Me (In Their Words)

Confirmation Of My Adherence To The Principles Of The Jury Team, Of The Correctness Of This Application And Of My Eligibility To Be A Member Of The Westminster Parliament

1. I agree not to support any policies discriminating on the basis of race, colour, gender, sexual orientation, disability or religious or other belief.

2. I shall support the three Jury Team Principles and all policies which lead to better governance of parliament and government. I shall commit to the Nolan Principles of Public Life: Selflessness, Integrity, Objectivity, Accountability, Openness, Honesty and Leadership.

3. I agree that if I reach the short-list for my Constituency then it will be necessary for me to be able to prove my credentials and to demonstrate my eligibility for election. I accept that to do so may require that I present to representatives of the Jury

Team evidence of my identification such as my passport or birth certificate, utility bills, driving licence (including counterpart) and other information relating to my education and career. I also agree to authorise the Jury Team to undertake an enhanced Criminal Records Bureau check on me. I agree that if the Jury Team, acting reasonably, are not content with and convinced by the information I shall provide to them to demonstrate the credentials shown on my application form above then I shall no longer be a valid candidate for the Jury Team.

4. I confirm that I shall use my savings or other resources to pay the election deposit (£500) for my nomination if I am selected (the Jury Team will assist in this in cases of genuine need).

5. I acknowledge that the Jury Team will be assisting me in being elected as a Member of the Westminster Parliament and in exchange for this assistance I hereby irrevocably agree that if elected to that Parliament:

   a. I shall undertake all of the necessary formalities to be properly accepted as a Member of the Westminster Parliament, including swearing the Oath of Allegiance, within three months of being elected or shall forthwith resign my seat in Parliament

   b. If the Jury Team, acting reasonably, determines that I have joined any other political party or similar grouping or that any of the information on this form is inaccurate or omits one or more significant factors about me then I shall forthwith resign my seat in Parliament.

6. I confirm that:

   a. I am 21 years old or over and am a British citizen or a citizen of another Commonwealth country or of the Irish Republic

   b. I am not a civil servant, a member of a police force, a member of the armed forces, a government nominated director of a commercial company, a judge or a member of the legislature of any country or territory outside the Commonwealth

c. I am not a peer who sits in the House of Lords by virtue of section 2 of the House of Lords Act 1999, i.e. who can vote in the House of Lords, or a bishop who is entitled to sit and vote in the House of Lords

d. I am not the subject of a bankruptcy restriction order in England or Wales, have not been adjudged bankrupt in Northern Ireland and have not had my estate sequestered in Scotland

e. I am not a convicted prisoner who is serving a prison sentence of more than 12 months (disqualification under Representation of the People Act 1981) and am not a person convicted of treason still undertaking my sentence

g. I have never been found guilty of corrupt or illegal practices in elections

I hereby confirm that to the best of my knowledge and belief all of the information in the form above, including that provided by my supporters, is correct and does not omit any matter which might embarrass the Jury Team.

Signed as a Deed by:

Name:

Date: Day: Month: Year:

Witnessed by:

Date: Day: Month: Year:

You Must Confirm This Signing And Pay The £25 Registration Fee:

Click Here:

INDEX

C

S